INFORMATION INDIA 1988

Global View

CONCEPTS IN COMMUNICATION INFORMATICS & LIBRARIANSHIP

[CICIL]

General Editor: **S.P. AGRAWAL**

CICIL-1
Development of Library Services in India: Social Science Information **S.P. Agrawal**

CICIL-2
Development of Documentation in India: Social Science Information **S.P. Agrawal**

CICIL-3
Unesco and Social Sciences: Retrospect and Prospect **S.P. Agrawal** and **J.C. Aggarwal**

CICIL-4
INDIANA: A Bibliography of Bibliographical Sources **M.K. Jain**

CICIL-5
Dimensions of Library and Information Science: Papers contributed in honour of the 61st birthday celebration of Prof. P.N. Kaula **V. Venkatappaiah** (Ed.) (in press)

CICIL-6
Book Numbers: Some Indian Methods **M.P. Satija** and **S.P. Agrawal** (in press)

CICIL-7
National Policy for University Libraries in India: Problems and Perspectives **N.B. Inamdar** and **L.S. Ramaiah**

CICIL-8
Media Utilisation for the Development of Women and Children **B.S. Thakur** and **Binod C. Agrawal** (in press)

CICIL-9
Terrorism: An Annotated Bibliography **Susheela Bhan** (in press)

CICIL-10
Transnational Library Relations: A Indo-American Experience **M.B. Konnur** (in press)

CICIL-11
Geography of Marketing and Commercial Activities in India (Decumentation on Research Information) **R.S. Dixit** (in press)

CICIL-12
Information India 1988: Global View **S.P. Agrawal** and **J.C. Aggarwal**

Concepts in Communication
Informatics & Librarianship-12

General Editor: **S.P. Agrawal**

Information India 1988

Global View

S.P. Agrawal
J.C. Aggarwal

CONCEPT PUBLISHING COMPANY, NEW DELHI-110059

ISBN 81-7022-275-3

First Published 1989

Published by

Ashok Kumar Mittal
Concept Publishing Company
A/15-16, Commercial Block, Mohan Garden
NEW DELHI - 110059 (India)

Lesertypeset by

Microtech Advance **Printing Systems (Pvt.) Ltd.**
H-13, Bali Nagar,
NEW DELHI - 110015

Printed by

D.B. Offset Works
B-218, Naraina Industrial Area,
NEW DELHI - 110028

CONTENTS

CONCEPT INFORMATION INDIA 1988

Global View

General Editor's Introduction

CICIL is a series launched by the publishers covering communication, information technology and librarianship fields which are interrelated and which at the same time, in themselves include in their scope a very wide stretch of topics for investigation, research and study.

Communication is a quality of the sentient. Home sapiens high up in the evolutionary order, had fashioned many modes and mediums of expression. Of late, technology has armed man with dynamic and effecting communication. All this necessitates us to reflect on the role of librarian in the emerging scenario. Librarianship, the grand discipline with the art and science of management, in a sense lords over all the subjects. The present series will look at ideas, old and new, in all the allied areas.

The focus of the book is on India as it was in 1988. As many as Eleven out of the total of Thirteen chapters are devoted to the various aspects of the country under suitable divisions. The chapters are a combination of descriptive accounts and statistics.

A geographical account of the land and its people is followed by a historical description of India since 1947. The next three chapters deal with the details of the country's economy from the successive Plans to agriculture, rural development and industries. Then follows education with enough data to stimulate the further pursuit of knowledge. The chapter on fiscal issues leaves nothing that is useful and includes information about excise and customs, money and banking, and subsidies for social justice.

Another chapter gives a lot of information about child labour, energy, health and nutrition, mass media and other topical issues, which are important in any discussion on India. Besides, the reader gets the entire range of information to be found in any standard year book. And all this information has been imported in the background of global data, giving an overview of the world at large.

S.P. Agrawal

Preface

In presenting this publication, we have been guided by the motto that 'information is public service'. Combining information technology and librarianship, we have endeavoured to give our readers more than a birds's eye view of India by itself and as part of the world as a whole. We have taken into account the various aspects of the development of India, with a focus on relevant and comparative data on the rest of the world.

To make the present volume worthwhile, we have included in it a comparative study of the indicators of development with regard to 161 countries, including different kinds of developed, developing and under-developed nations.

A word about Country-profiles, statistics for various countries, taken from different sources, do not necessarily relate to the same year in some cases.

In so far as India is concerned, we have placed at the disposal of our readers the useful statistics relating to the various sectors of development since 1947. The chapter on the major events of the year gives a panoramic view of almost everything important that happened in India.

We are confident that this publication will serve to fill up the need for a reliable reference manual, which will come handy to a large number of readers spread over different disciplines — administrators, legislators, research workers, writers and those trying to drink deep from the ocean of knowledge.

S.P. AGRAWAL
J.C. AGGARWAL

CHAPTER 1

OVERVIEW : NATIONAL - INTERNATIONAL

I.1 DEMOGRAPHIC DATA

Item	India	Best Country/ Countries	No. of Countries for which Data Available	India's Position in the World
1. Population Annual Growth Rate % 1980-86	2.2	-0.1 Hungary and German Democratic Republic	126	51
2. Crude Death Rate 1987	11	0.3 Kuwait	131	52
3. Crude Birth Rate 1987	32	Italy 11 Denmark11 Sweden 11	131	69
4. Life Expectancy 1987	59	Japan 78 years	131	47
5. Total Fertility Rate	4.2	Germany, Fed. Republic of 1.4	131	66
6. % Population Urbanised	27	Singapore 100 Belgium 97 Kuwait 95 Hong Kong 93 United Kingdom 92	131	27

I.2 ECONOMIC DATA

Item	Year	India	Country at the Top	Countries for which Data Available	India's Position in the World
1. G.N.P. Per Capita (U.S. Dollars)	1986	290	Switzerland 17680	120	97
2. % Rate of Inflation	1980-86	7.8	-1.4 United Arab Emirates	112	72
3. % Population Below Poverty Line	1977-86				
a) Urban		40		47	29
b) Rural		51			
4. % of Expenditure on	1986				
(a) Health		2.1	17.9 German Fed.Rep. of	72	64
(b) Education		2.1	23.9 Ghana	74	71
(c) Defence		18.4	60 Yugoslavia	70	16

I.3 EDUCATION DATA

Item	India	Country with Best Position	Countries for which Data Available	India's Position in the World
1. Adult Literacy (1985)				
(a) Male	57	98 Italy	100	69
(b) Female	29	96 1. Chile 2. Cuba 3. Italy	100	73
2. Primary School Enrolment Ratio 1984-86 (gross)				
(a) Male	107	137 China	122	28
(b) Female ('Net' in the case of India not available)	76	127 Lesotho	122	86
3. % of Grade 1 Enrolment Completing Primary School (1980-1986)	38 (1978)	100 1. Norway 2. Japan	116	89
4. Secondary School Enrolment Ratio 1984-1986 (gross)				
(a) Male	45	1. 100 U.S.A. 2. 105 Denmark		Male 62 Female 80
(b) Female	24	3. 103 Canada 4. 106 Netherland 1. 100 U.S.A. 2. 101 Ireland 3. 101 Spain 4. 103 Canada 5. 102 Netherlands 6. 100 Norway 7. 110 Finland		

I.4 HEALTH DATA

Item	India	Country with Best Position	Countries for which Data Available	India's Position in the World
1. % of Population with Access to Drinking Water 1980-87 (a) Total (b) Urban (c) Rural	(a) 56 (b) 80 (c) 47	100 Kuwait and Singapore	91	37
2. % of Population with Access to Health Services 1980-87	–	100 Kuwait, Mauritius Singapore	71	–
3. Percentage Duly Immunized 1981/1986-87 One Year Old Children				
TB	12/46	100/97 Chile	101	87
DPT	31/58	99/99 Sweden	128	73
Polio	7/50	99/98 Sweden	128	90
Measeles	./17	99/99 Hungary	103	118
4. % Births Attended by Trained Health Personnel 1983-87	33	100 USSR Bulgaria Czechoslovakia Belgium, U.S.A. Norway, Sweden	90	64
5. Maternal Mortality Rate 1980-87	500	02 Canada 04 Hongkong Norway Sweden	107	93

I.5 NUTRITION DATA

	Item	India	Country with Best Position	Countries for which Data Available	India's Position in the world
1.	% of Children with Low Birth Weight 1982-87	30	4 Ireland, Hong Kong, Sweden	121	118
2.	% of Children under five Suffering from Malnutrition (1980-86) (a) Mild-Moderate (b) Severe	(a) 33 (b) 05	Figures available for a few countries only		
3.	Average Index of Food Production Per Capita (1979-81 = 100) 1986	111	202 Saudi Arabia 143 Hong Kong	128	23
4.	Daily Per Capita Calorie supply as % of Requirements 1985	94	152 Libyan Arab Jamahiriya 146 Bulgaria 145 Greece	128	91
5.	% of Household Income spent on all Food 1980-85	52	2 Canada 4 Denmark, Hon Kong, Norway and Sweden	Data of many countries not available	

I.6 DATA ON DIVERSE ISSUES
(i) Children and Women Data

	Item	India	Country with Best Position	Countries for which Data Available	India's Position in the World
1.	Under 5 Mortality Rate (1987)	152	07 Sweden	130	92
2.	Infant Mortality Rate Under I (1987)	100	05 Japan	130	92
3.	% Contraceptive Prevalence 1981-85	34	83 United Kingdom	104	56
4.	% Pregnant Women immunized against Tetanus 1986-87	47	90 Costa Rica Singapore Hong Kong	Information of many advanced countries not available	
5.	Adult Literacy Rate as Percentage of Males 1985	50.9	—	Information of many advanced countries not available	

(ii) G.N.P. Per Capita Under 5 Mortality Rate and Literacy Rate 1986-87

Country	*G.N.P. 1986*	*U5MR 1987*	*Literacy Rate in percentage*
1. Brazil	1,810	87	79
2. Cameroon	910	156	62
3. China	300	45	69
4. **India**	290	152	43
5. Italy	8,550	12	97
6. Libya (1985)	7,170	123	66
7. Oman	4,980	149	30
8. Singapore	7,410	12	86
9. Spain	4,860	11	95
10. South Africa	2,010	101	—
11. Sri Lanka	400	45	87
12. Trinidad	5,360	24	96
13. UAE	14,680	33	53
14. U.S.A.	17,480	13	99
15. U.S.S.R. (1980)	4,550	30	100
16. Yugoslavia	2,300	28	92
17. Zambia	300	130	76

(iii) Central Revenues (1986) Percentage of Current Revenue

Country		Taxes on Income Profit and Capital Gain	Social Security Contribution	Domestic Taxes on Goods	Taxes on International Trade and Transactions	Other Taxes	Non-Tax Revenue	Total Current Revenue (percentage of G.N.P.)
1. Canada	49.3	14.5	18.5	4.7	0.0	13.0	19.7	
2. **India**	14.8	—	38.0	26.9	0.4	19.9	13.3	
3. Pakistan	11.9	—	33.0	31.0	0.3	23.8	16.2	
4. Sweden	16.0	29.8	29.6	0.5	8.3	15.8	41.1	
5. United Kingdom	38.9	17.5	30.4	0.0	1.9	11.4	37.9	
6. United States	50.1	33.9	3.9	1.7	0.8	9.5	19.5	

(iv) Central Expenditure

(Percentage of Total Expenditure)

Country	Defence	Education	Health	Housing Social Security	Economic Services	Others	Total Expenditure (% of G.N.P.)	Overall Surplus/ Deficit (% of G.N.P.)
1. Canada	7.6	3.4	6.1	35.0	14.9	33.1	25.4	-6.2
2. **India**	18.4	2.1	2.1	5.6	23.4	48.5	16.4	-8.1
3. Pakistan	33.9	3.2	1.0	10.5	25.8	25.6	23.1	-9.5
4. Sweden	6.6	8.9	1.1	51.8	6.8	24.8	44.1	-1.2
5. United Kingdom	13.3	2.1	12.6	30.2	8.9	33.0	40.6	-2.7
6. United States	25.8	1.7	11.6	31.0	8.8	21.1	24.5	-5.0

(v) Investment, Savings and Inflation

Country	Ratio of Investment to G.D.P.		Ratio of Savings to G.D.P.		Rate of Inflation	
	Average 1976-80	Average 1981-85	Average 1976-80	Average 1981-83	Average 1976-80	Average 1981-85
1. Burma	17.1	22.3	14.0	18.1	4.3	4.6
2. China	33.3	30.3	33.2	30.0	3.3	3.5
3. Hong Kong	—	28.4	32.1	30.3	9.0	9.2
4. **India**	23.0	24.0	22.1	21.4	4.2	9.3
5. Republic of Korea	30.3	27.9	26.2	23.3	17.4	7.3
6. Pakistan	16.3	17.3	13.4	13.9	8.7	7.3
7. Singapore	40.8	44.7	31.4	36.5	3.7	3.3
8. Sri Lanka	22.0	27.5	15.4	11.0	10.3	12.2
9. Thailand	26.8	22.4	20.9	18.5	9.8	5.0
10. Turkey	23.0	20.2	17.0	17.1	13.2	10.8

(Source: World Economic Survey 1987)

(vi) Labour Force and Urbanization 1985

Percentage of Population of Working Age (15-64 years)

India	China	Pakistan	Japan	Canada	Netherland	Germany
56	65	53	68	68	69	Fed. Rep. of 70 (maximum)
United States		Switzerland		United Kingdom		
66		67		65		–

Urbanization

Percentage of Total Population 1985

India	China	Pakistan	Japan	Canada	Netherlands	Germany, Fed.
25	22	29	76	77	88	Rep. of 86
United States	Switzerland	United Kingdom	USSR	Hongkong	Singapore	Belgium
74	60	92	66	93	100	96

(vii) Unemployment Rate (1987)

Percentage of Total Labour Force - Estimates)

Australia	Austria	Belgium	Canada	Denmark	Finland	France
8.1	3.9	10.9	8.8	8.5	5.0	10.8
Germany, Fed.	Greece	Iceland	Ireland	Italy	Japan	Luxembourg
Rep. of 6.5	8.7	0.7	18.7	11.5	2.8	1.2
Netherlands	New Zealand	Norway	Portugal	Spain	Sweden	Switzerland
9.6	5.7	2.1	8.7	21.1	1.9	0.8
United Kingdom		United States				
10.3		6.1				

(*Source*: *World Economic Survey 1988*)

(viii) Production 1986

(Million of Dollars)

Country	G.D.P. (Gross Domestic Production)	Distribution of Gross Domestic Product (Percent)			
		Agriculture	Industry	Manufacturing	Services
1. **India**	203,790	32	29	19	39
2. Pakistan	30,080	24	28	17	47
3. China	271,880	31	46	34	23
4. U.K.	468,290	02	43	26	55
5. Canada	323,790	03	36	—	61
6. Sweden	114,470	03	35	24	62

Note: Manufacturing being the most dynamic part of the industrial sector, its share of G.D.P. is shown separately.

(ix) Crude Oil in Developing Countries

(Millions of Barrels)

OPEC Countries 6459.0/Non-OPEC Developing Countries 2982.5

Oil-Exporting Developing Countries (2332.3)		Energy-Deficient Developing Countries 650.2	
1. Angola	124.6	Argentina	153.0
2. Bahrain	15.8	Bangladesh	0.2
3. Bolivia	6.8	Barbados	0.5
4. Brunei Darusalam	48.8	Benin	4.4
5. Cameroon	62.1	Brazil	205.4
6. Colombia	141.5	Burma	8.8
7. Congo	43.1	Chile	10.3
8. Egypt	328.2	Cote d' Ivoire	5.8
9. Malaysia	170.6	Cuba	7.3
10. Mexico	926.3	Guatemala	1.4
11. Oman	206.2	**India**	222.2
12. Peru	0.8	Jordan	0.1
13. Syrian Arab Republic	84.6	Morocco	15.2
14. Trinidad and Tobago	59.5	Pakistan	10.9
15. Tunisia	38.1	Philippines	0.8
16. Yemen	3.7	Suriname	11.4
17. Zaire	11.6	Thailand	

Source: *World Economic Survey 1988*

CHAPTER 2

COMPARATIVE COUNTRY PROFILE

II.1 DEMOGRAPHIC DATA

	Total Population (in millions) 1987	Population Annual Rate	Crude Death Growth Rate 1987 % 1980-86	Crude Birth Rate 1987	Life Expectancy 1987 1987	Total Fertility Rate urbanised	% Population 1987
1	2	3	4	5	6	7	8
1. Afghanistan	14.7	—	23	49	42	6.9	21
2. Albania	3.1	2.1	06	24	72	2.9	35
3. Algeria	23.1	3.1	09	40	63	5.7	44
4. Angola	9.2	2.6	20	47	45	6.4	26
5. Argentina	31.1	1.6	09	22	71	2.9	85
6. Australia	16.2	1.4	07	15	76	1.8	85
7. Austria	7.5	0.0	12	12	74	1.5	57
8. Bangladesh	106.7	2.6	16	42	52	5.4	13
9. Balgium	9.9	0.0	11	12	75	1.6	97
10. Benin	4.3	3.2	19	50	47	7.0	38
11. Bhutan	1.4	2.0	17	38	49	5.5	05
12. Bolivia	6.7	2.7	14	43	54	6.0	49
13. Botswana	1.2	3.5	12	48	59	6.1	21
14. Brazil	145.5	2.2	08	29	65	3.3	75
15. Bulgaria	9.0	0.2	12	13	72	1.9	68
16. Burkina Faso	8.3	2.5	19	47	48	6.5	08
17. Burma	39.1	2.0	10	31	61	3.9	24
18. Burundi	5.0	2.7	17	46	50	6.2	06

(Contd.) Table I.1

Table II.1 (Contd.)

1	2	3	4	5	6	7	8
19. Cameroon	10.4	3.2	16	42	52	5.8	46
20. Canada	25.9	1.1	07	14	77	1.7	76
21. Central African Republic	2.7	2.5	20	44	46	5.8	44
22. Chad	5.3	2.3	20	44	46	5.8	30
23. Chile	12.5	1.7	06	24	72	2.7	84
24. China	1088.6	1.2	07	20	70	2.3	21
25. Colombia	29.9	1.9	07	29	65	3.5	69
26. Congo	18.0	3.3	17	44	49	5.9	41
27. Costa Rica	2.8	2.4	04	28	75	3.2	51
28. Cote d' Ivoire	11.1	4.2	14	51	53	7.4	44
29. Cuba	10.1	0.9	07	16	74	1.7	73
30. Czechoslovakia	15.6	0.3	12	14	72	2.0	67
31. Denmark	5.1	0.0	11	11	76	1.5	86
32. Dominican Rep.	6.7	2.4	07	32	67	3.6	58
33. Ecquador	9.9	2.9	08	36	66	4.5	54
34. Egypt	50.2	2.7	10	36	62	4.6	48
35. El Salvodor	4.9	1.2	09	36	64	4.7	44
36. Ethiopia	43.8	2.4	24	44	42	6.2	12
37. Finland	4.9	0.5	10	13	75	1.7	65
38. France	55.6	0.5	10	14	76	1.8	74
39. Gabon	1.1	4.4	17	38	52	5.1	43
40. German Dem. Rep.	16.6	-0.1	13	13	74	1.7	77

(Contd.) Table I.1

Table II.1 (Contd.

1	2	3	4	5	6	7	8
41. Germany, Fed. Rep. of	60.8	0.2	12	10	75	1.4	86
42. Ghana	13.7	3.5	13	44	55	6.3	32
43. Greece	10.0	0.5	10	12	76	1.7	61
44. Guatemala	8.4	2.9	09	41	63	5.6	41
45. Guinea	6.4	2.4	22	47	43	6.1	24
46. Guinea-Bissau	0.9	—	20	41	46	5.4	29
47. Guyana	1.0	—	05	25	70	2.6	33
48. Haiti	6.1	1.8	13	34	55	4.6	29
49. Honduras	4.7	3.6	08	40	65	5.3	41
50. Hong Kong (colony)	5.6	1.2	06	16	76	1.7	93
51. Hungary	10.6	-0.1	13	12	71	1.8	58
52. **India**	802.1	2.2	11	32	59	4.2	27
53. Indonesia	172.2	2.2	11	28	57	3.1	27
54. Iran, Islamic Rep. of	51.3	2.8	08	42	66	5.6	53
55. Iraq	17.1	3.6	08	43	65	6.2	72
56. Irland	3.6	-0.8	09	18	74	2.4	58
57. Israel	4.4	1.7	07	22	76	2.8	91
58. Italy	57.2	0.3	10	11	76	1.5	68
59. Jamaica	2.8	1.5	06	26	74	2.7	51
60. Japan	121.9	0.7	07	12	78	1.7	77
61. Jordan	3.8	3.7	07	46	67	7.1	66
62. Kampuchea	7.7	—	17	42	49	4.6	11

(Contd.) Table I.1

Table II.1 (Contd.)

1	2	3	4	5	6	7	8
63. Kenya	22.1	4.1	12	54	59	7.9	22
64. Korea, Dem. Rep. of	21.4	2.5	05	29	70	3.5	65
65. Korea, Rep. of	42.1	1.4	06	19	70	1.9	68
66. Kuwait	2.4	4.4	03	33	73	4.6	95
67. Lao People's Dem. Rep.	3.8	2.0	17	42	49	5.6	17
68. Lebanon	2.8	—	08	29	68	3.3	83
69. Lesotho	1.6	2.7	13	41	57	5.7	18
70. Liberia	2.3	3.3	13	45	55	6.3	32
71. Libyan Arab Jamahiriya	4.1	3.9	10	44	62	6.8	67
72. Madagascar	10.9	3.3	14	46	54	6.6	23
73. Malawai	7.6	3.2	20	53	48	7.0	13
74. Malaysia	16.2	2.7	06	29	70	3.3	40
75. Mali	8.6	2.3	21	50	45	6.7	19
76. Mauritania	1.9	2.6	19	46	47	6.5	38
77. Mauritius	1.1	1.0	05	19	69	1.9	42
78. Mexico	83.0	2.2	06	29	69	3.4	71
79. Mangolia	2.0	2.8	08	39	64	5.3	51
80. Morocco	23.3	2.5	10	36	62	4.6	46
81. Mozambique	14.5	2.7	19	45	47	6.3	23
82. Nepal	17.8	2.6	15	40	52	5.8	09
83. Netherlands	14.5	0.5	09	12	77	1.5	89
84. New Zealand	3.3	0.9	08	16	75	1.9	84
85. Nicaragua	3.5	3.4	08	42	64	5.3	58

(Contd.) Table I.1

Table II.1 (Contd.

1	2	3	4	5	6	7	8
86. Niger	6.5	3.0	21	51	45	7.1	18
87. Nigeria	101.9	3.3	16	50	51	6.9	33
88. Norway	4.2	0.3	11	12	77	1.7	73
89. Oman	1.3	4.7	13	46	57	7.1	10
90. Pakistan	111.0	3.1	13	47	58	6.3	31
91. Panama	2.3	2.2	05	27	72	3.0	53
92. Papua New Guinea	3.7	2.1	12	39	55	5.5	15
93. Paraguay	3.9	3.2	07	35	67	4.5	46
94. Peru	20.7	2.3	09	35	63	4.3	69
95. Philippines	58.0	2.5	08	33	64	4.2	41
96. Poland	103.0	0.9	10	17	72	2.2	62
97. Portugal	10.2	0.5	10	14	74	1.7	32
98. Romania	22.9	0.5	11	16	71	2.1	50
99. Rwanda	6.5	3.3	17	51	49	8.2	07
100. Saudi Arabia	12.6	4.1	08	42	64	7.1	75
101 Senegal	6.8	2.9	19	46	47	6.3	37
102. Sierra Leone	3.8	2.4	24	48	42	6.5	30
103. Singapore	2.6	1.1	06	17	73	1.7	100
104. Somalia	6.9	2.9	20	51	46	6.6	34
105. South Africa	33.0	2.2	10	32	61	4.4	57
106. Spain	38.9	0.6	09	13	77	1.7	77
107. Sri Lanka	16.6	1.5	06	23	71	2.6	21
108. Suden	23.1	2.8	16	45	51	6.4	21
109. Sweden	8.3	0.1	12	11	77	1.7	84

(Contd.) Table II.1

Table II.1. (Contd.)

1	2	3	4	5	6	7	8
110. Switzerland	6.5	0.3	11	12	77	1.7	73
111. Syrian Arab Rep.	11.2	3.5	07	44	66	6.6	51
112. Tanzania, U. Rep. of	24.5	3.5	14	51	54	7.1	28
113. Thailand	53.3	2.0	07	23	66	2.4	21
114. Togo	33.1	3.4	14	45	54	6.0	24
115. Trinidad and Tobago	1.2	1.5	07	24	71	2.6	66
116. Tunisia	7.6	2.3	07	31	66	3.8	54
117. Turkey	52.5	2.5	08	29	65	3.4	47
118. Uganda	16.6	3.1	16	50	52	6.9	10
119. USSR	281.5	1.0	11	18	70	2.3	66
120. United Arab Emirates	1.5	5.6	04	23	71	4.6	77
121. United Kingdom	56.7	0.1	12	13	76	1.8	92
122. U.S.A.	243.4	1.0	09	15	76	1.8	74
123. Uruguay	3.1	0.4	10	19	71	2.6	85
124. Venezuela	18.3	2.9	05	31	70	3.6	89
125. Vietnam	62.8	2.6	10	32	62	3.9	21
126. Yemen	7.3	3.1	16	48	52	6.9	22
127. Yemen, Dem.	2.3	2.5	16	47	52	6.6	42
128. Yugoslavia	23.4	0.7	09	15	72	1.9	48
129. Zaira	32.7	3.1	14	46	53	6.1	38
130. Zambia	7.6	3.5	14	51	54	7.1	52
131. Zimbabwe	8.8	3.7	10	42	59	5.6	26

II.2 ECONOMIC DATA

	GNP Per Capita (U.S. $) 1986	Rate of Inflation (%) 1980-86	% of Population below absolute Poverty Line 1977-1986 Urban/Rural		% of Central Govt. Expenditure allocated to Health/ Education/ Defence		
1	2	3	4		5		
1. Afghanistan	—	10.5	50	68	5.0	12.1	9.7
2. Albania	—	—					
3. Algeria	2590	6.1	20	—	—	—	—
4. Angola	470 (1980)	—	—	—	—	—	—
5. Argentia	2350	326.2	—	—	1.3	6.0	5.2
6. Australia	11920	8.2	—	—	9.5	7.2	9.3
7. Austria	9990	4.5	—	—	12.0	9.7	3.1
8. Bangladesh	160	11.2	86	86	5.3	9.9	11.2
9. Belgium	9230	5.7	—	—	1.7	13.0	5.3
10. Benin	270	8.6	—	65	—	—	—
11. Bhutan	150	—	—	—	—	—	—
12. Bolivia	600	683.7	—	85 (1975)	1.4	11.6	5.8
13. Botswana	840	7.6	40	55	5.0	17.7	6.4
14. Brazil	1810	14.9	20	32	7.5	17.5	28.7
15. Bulgaria	4150 (1980)	—	—	—	—	—	—
16. Burkina Faso	150	6.3	—	—	—	—	—
17. Burma	200	2.1	40	40	7.7	11.7	18.8
18. Burundi	240	6.4	55	85	—	—	—

(Contd.) Table II.2

Table II.2 (Contd.)

1	2	3	4		5		
19. Cameroon	910	11.0	15	40	5.1	14.4	8.8
20. Canada	14120	5.5	-	-	6.1	3.4	7.6
21. Central African Republic	290	11.5	-	91	-	-	-
22. Chad	80	-	30	56	-	-	-
	(1982)	-	(1982)	(1982)			
23. Chile	1320	20.2	27	-	6.0	12.5	10.7
24. China	300	3.8	-	10	-	-	-
25. Colombia	1230	22.6	32	-	-	-	-
26. Congo	990	7.5	-	-	-	-	-
27. Costa Rica	1480	32.3	-	-	19.3	16.3	16.2
28. Cote d' Ivoire	730	8.3	30	26	4.0	20.5	3.9
29. Cuba	2070	31.2	-	-	-	-	-
30. Czechoslovakia	5820 (1980)	-	-	-	-	-	-
31. Denmark	2600	7.3	-	-	10.0	6.2	4.4
32. Dominican Rep.	710	15.9	45	43	9.0	12.8	8.1
33. Ecuador	1160	29.5	40	65	7.3	24.5	11.8
34. Egypt	760	12.4	41	25	2.4	10.8	17.7
35. El Salvador	820	14.9	20	32	7.5	17.5	28.7
36. Ethiopia	120	3.4	60	65	-	-	-
37. Finland	12160	8.1	-	-	10.6	13.7	5.2
38. France	10720	8.8	-	-	-	-	
39. Gabon	3080	4.8	65	80	-	-	-
40. German Dem. Republic	7180 (1980)	-	-	-	-	-	-

(Contd.) Table II.2

Table II.2 (Contd.)

1	2	3	4		5		
41. Germany, Fed. Republic of	12080	3.0	-	-	17.9	0.6	8.8
42. Ghana	390	50.8	59	37	8.3	23.9	6.5
43. Greece	3680	20.3	-	-	-	-	-
44. Guatemala	930	11.3	66	74	-	-	-
45. Guinea	-	-	-	-	-	-	-
46. Guinea-Bissau	170	30.4	-	-	-	14.0	-
47. Guyana	500	9.4	-	-	2.0	3.0	-
48. Haiti	330	7.7					
49. Honduras	740	5.2	14	55	-	-	-
50 Hong Kong (colony)	6910	6.9	-	-	-	-	-
51. Hungary	2020	15.4	-	-	3.6	1.6	6.9
52. **India**	290	7.8	40	51	2.1	2.1	18.4
53. Indonesia	490	8.9	26	44	1.9	8.5	9.3
54. Iran, Islamic Rep. of	-	-	-	-	-	-	-
55. Iraq	3020 (1980)	-	-	-	-	-	-
56. Ireland	5070	10.7	-	-	13.2	11.7	3.1
57. Israel	6210	182.9	-	-	3.4	6.7	30.1
58. Italy	8550	13.2	-	-	9.9	7.2	3.2
59. Jamaica	840	19.8	-	80	-	-	-
60. Japan	12840	1.6	-	-	-	-	-
61. Jordan	1540	3.2	14	17	3.8	12.2	26.7
62. Kampuchea	-	-	-	-	-	-	-
63. Kenya	300	9.9	10	55	6.4	19.7	8.7

(Contd.) Table II.2

Table II.2 (Contd.)

1	2	3	4		5		
64. Korea, Dem. Rep. of	-	-	-	-	-	-	-
65. Korea, Rep. of	2370	5.4	18	11	15.0	18.1	29.2
66. Kuwait	13890	-	-	-	7.1	13.4	0.8
67. Lao People's Dem. Rep.	-	-	-	-	-	-	-
68. Lebanon	-	-	-	-	-	-	-
69. Lesotho	370	13.1	50	55	6.9	15.5	9.6
70. Liberia	460	1.1	-	23	5.7	14.2	7.7
71. Libyan Arab Jamahiriya	-	-	-	-	-	-	-
72. Madagascar	230	17.8	50	50			
73. Malawi	160	12.4	25	85	6.9	11.0	6.0
74. Malaysia	1830	1.4	13	38	-	-	-
75. Mali	180	7.4	27	48	1.7	9.0	8.1
76. Mauritania	420	9.9	-	-	-	-	-
77. Mauritius	1200	8.1	12	12	7.7	13.4	0.8
78. Mexico	1860	63.7	-	-	-	-	-
79. Mongolia	-	-	-	-	-	-	-
80. Morocco	590	7.7	28	45	2.8	16.6	16.4
81. Mozambique	210	28.1	-	-	-	-	-
82. Nepal	150	8.8	55	61	5.0	12. 1	6.2
83. Netherlands	10020	3.1	-	-	10.8	11.1	5.2
84. New Zealand	7460	11.0	-	-	12.5	10.9	4.7
85. Nicaragua	790	56.5	21	19	-	-	-
86. Niger	260	6.6	21	35	-	-	-

(Contd.) Table II.2

Table II.2 (Contd.)

1	2	3	4		5		
87. Nigeria	640	10.5	-	-	-	-	-
88. Norway	15400	7.0	-	-	10.5	8.7	8.3
89. Oman	4980	3.6	-	-	5.0	10.1	41.9
90. Pakistan	350	7.5	32	29	10.0	3.2	33.9
91. Panama	2330	3.3	21	30	15.8	16.0	-
92. Papua New Guinea	720	5.1	10	75	9.6	17.0	4.5
93. Paraguay	1000	19.1	19	50	3.1	12.2	12.1
94. Peru	760	12.4	21	25	2.4	10.8	17.7
95. Philippines	560	18.2	50	64	1.4	11.5	2.5
96. Poland	2070	31.2	-	-	-	-	-
97. Portugal	2250	22.0	-	-	-	-	-
98. Romania	2560	-	-	-	-	-	60.0
99. Rwanda	290	5.6	30 (1975)	90	-	-	-
100. Saudi Arabia	6950	-1.3	-	-	-	-	-
101. Senegal	420	9.5	-	-	-	-	-
102. Sierra Leone	310	33.5	-	65	5.8	12.8	3.4
103. Singapore	7410	1.9	-	-	6.5	21.6	22.5
104. Somalia	280	45.4	40	70	-	-	-
105. South Africa	1850	13.6	-	-	-	-	-
106. Spain	4860	11.3	-	-	13.1	6.2	4.4
107. Sri Lanka	400	13.5	-	-	8.1	19.8	4.9
108. Sudan	320	32.6	-	85	-	-	-
109. Sweden	13160	8.2	-	-	1.1	8.9	6.6

(Contd.) Table II.2

Table II.2 (Contd.)

1	2	3	4		5		
110. Switzerland	17680	4.2	-	-	13.1	3.1	10.3
111. Syrian Arab Rep.	1570	-	-	-	-	-	-
112. Tanzania, U. Rep. of	250	21.5	-	-	4.9	7.2	13.8
113. Thailand	810	3.0	15	34	5.7	19.5	20.2
114. Togo	250	6.7	42	-	3.6	11.7	6.9
115. Trinidad and Tobago	5360	8.6	-	39	-	-	-
116. Tunisia	1140	8.9	20	15	6.5	14.3	7.9
117. Turkey	1110	37.3	-	-	2.2	11.9	13.5
118. Uganda	230	74.9	-	-	2.4	15.0	26.3
119. USSR	4550	-	-	-	-	-	-
120. United Arab Emirates	14680	-1.4	-	-	6.2	9.7	45.3
121. United Kingdom	8870	6.0	-	-	12.6	2.1	13.3
122. U.S.A	17480	4.4	-	-	11.6	1.7	25.8
123. Uruguay	1900	50.4	22	-	4.8	7.1	10.2
124. Venezuela	2920	8.7	-	-	8.1	19.8	4.9
125. Vietnam	-	-	-	-	-	-	-
126. Yemen	550	13.1	-	-	4.7	22.5	28.8
127. Yemn. Dem.	470	4.8	20	-	-	-	
128. Yugoslavia	2300	51.8	+80 (1975)	-	-	-	60.0
129. Zaire	160	54.1					
130. Zambia	300	23.3	25	-	7.2	16.0	-
131. Zimbabwe	620	13.0	-	-	6.2	20.9	15.2

II.3 EDUCATION DATA

	Adult Literary Rate (1985)		Primary School Enrolment, Ratio 1984-86 (Net)		% of Grade Enrolment Completing Primary School 1980-86	Secondary School enrolment Ratio 1984-86	
	Male	Female	Male	Female		Male	Female
1	2		3		4	5	
1. Afghanistan	39	08	-	-	54	09	04
2. Albania	-	-	-	-	-	74	65
3. Algeria	63	37	96	80	83	62	45
4. Angola	49	-	71	61 (1982)	24	-	-
5. Argentina	96	95	-	-	66	68	79
6. Australia	-	-	97	98	-	95	98
7. Austria	-	-	-	-	95	78	80
8. Bangladesh	43	22	61	44	20	24	11
9. Belgium	99	99	94	96	75	95	97
10. Benin	37	16	68	34	15	23	09
11.Bhutan	-	-	-	-	25 (1978)	07	01
12. Bolivia	84	65	83	75 (1976)	32	40	34
13. Botswana	73	69	85	93	80	29	33
14. Brazil	79	76	-	-	20	-	-
15. Bulgaria	14	-	-	-	87	99	100
16. Burkina Faso	21	06	38	22	75	08	04
17. Burma	-	-	-	-	27	-	-
18. Burundi	43	26	46	37	-	06	03

(Contd.) Table II.3

Table II.3 (Contd.)

1	2		3		4	5	
19. Cameroon	68	55	-	-	70	29	18
20. Canada	-	-	97	96	-	103	103
21. Central African Republic	53	29	63	40	53	19	07
22. Chad	40	11	-	-	29 (1975)	10	02
23. Chile	97	96 (1983)	-	-	-	67	73
24. China	82	56	91	91	66	48	35
25. Colombia	89	87	72	74	37 (1973)	55	56
26. Congo	71	55	-	-	74	-	-
27. Costa Rica	94	93	87	88	75	41	44
28. Cote d' Ivoire	53	31	-	-	89 (1978)	27	12
29. Cuba	96	96	95	94	86	84	89
30. Czechoslovakia	-	-	-	-	94	-	-
31. Denmark	-	-	-	-	99	105	105
32. Dominican Rep.	78	77	80	78	88	43	56
33. Ecuador	85	80	-	-	50 (1983)	51 (1983)	53
34. Egypt	59	30	-	-	64	77	54
35. El Salvador	75	69	61	62	68	23	26
36. Ethiopia	-	-	-	-	41	14	09
37. Finland	-	-	-	-	-	95	110
38. France	-	-	100	100	95	92	99
39. Gabon	70	53-	-	-	59	31	32
40. German Dem. Rep.	-	-	-	-	-	79	70
41. Germany Fed. Rep. of	-	-	-	-	99	105	105

(Contd.) Table II.3

Table II.3 (Contd.)

1	2		3		4	5	
42. Ghana	64	43	-	-	75 (1977)	45	27
43. Greece	97	98	91	092	93	89	80
44. Guatemala	63	47	-	-	38	-	-
45. Guinea	40	17	30	14	37	14	05
46. Guinea-Bissau	46	17	71	35	18	18	04
47. Guyana	97	95	-	-	84 (1980)	58	62
48. Haiti	40	35	45	42	45 (1978)	19	17
49. Honduras	61	58	-	-	27	31	36
50. Hong Kong (colony)	95	81	95	95	98	66	72
51. Hungary	-	-	95	97	93	70	71
52. **India**	57	29	-	-	38 (1978)	45	24
53. Indonesia	83	65	99	97	80	45	34
54. Iran, Islamic Rep. of	62	39	99	90	70 (1969)	56	38
55. Iraq	90	87	92	81	65	65	39
56. Ireland	-	-	-	-	-	91	101
57. Israel	97	93	-	-	-	75	83
58. Italy	98	96	97	98	99	74	74
59. Jamaica	-	-	93	96	80 (1983)	56	60
60. Japan	-	-	100	100	100	95	97
61. Jordan	87	63	88	88	97 (1983)	80 (1983)	78
62. Kampuchea	85	85	-	-	40	26	11
63. Kenya	70	49	-	-	62	25	15
64. Korea, Rep. of	96	88	92	92	94	97	92
65. Kuwait	76	63	81	80	98	84	79

(Contd.) Table II.3

Table II.3 (Contd.)

1	2		3		4	5	
66. Lao People's Dem. Rep.	92	76	-	-	14	23	16
67. Lebanon	86	69	-	-	66	57	66
68. Lesotho	62	84	-	-	27	18	26
69. Liberia	47	23	-	-	-	33 (1980)	13
70. Libyan Arab Jamahiriya	81	50	-	-	82	-	-
71. Madagascar	74	62	-	-	30	43	30
72. Malawi	52	31	48	43	28	06	03
73. Malaysia	81	66	-	-	97	59	59
74. Mali	23	11	-	-	25	09	04
75. Mauritius	89	77	91	92	-	53	49
76. Mexico	92	88	-	-	66	56	54
77. Mongolia	93	86 (1982)	-	-	95 (1983)	88	96
78. Morocco	45	22	75	50	70	39	27
79. Mozambique	55	22	52	44	26	09	05
80. Nepal	39	12	76	35	27	35	11
81. Netherlands	-	-	85	88	95	106	102
82. New Zealand	-	-	100	100	-	83	96
83. Nicaragua	-	-	72	77	27	27	57
84. Niger	19	09	-	-	67 (1977)	09	03
85. Nigeria	54	31	-	-	31	42 (1976)	14
86. Norway	-	-	97	97	100	95	100
86A. Oman	47	12 (1982)	84	76	60 (1977)	45	25
87. Pakistan	40	19	-	-	34	25	10
88. Panama	89	98	90	89	73	56	63

(Contd.) Table II.3)

Table II.3 (Contd.)

1	2		3		4	5	
89. Papua New Guinea	55	35	-	-	67	20	15
90. Paraguay	91	85	86	84	48 (1977)	30	29
91. Peru	91	78	-	-	51	68	61
92. Philippines	86	85	95	94	64	66	69
93. Poland	-	-	-	-	94	78	81
94. Portugal	89	80	-	-	88 (1974)	47	56
95. Romania	-	-	-	-	98	84	80
96. Rowanda	61	33	65	63	47	04	02
97. Saudi Arabia	71 (1982)	31	64	48	79	52	35
98. Senegal	37	19	52	36	86	18	09
99. Sierrca Leone	38	21	-	-	48 (1982)	23 (1982)	11
100. Singapore	93	79	100	100	90	70	73
101. Somalia	18	06	19	10	33	15	08
102. South Africa	-	-	-	-	-	-	-
103. Spain	97	92	98	98	95	95	101
104. Sri Lanka	91	83	99	99	91	63	70
105. Sudan	33 (1986)	14	-	-	61	23	17
106. Sweden	-	-	-	-	98	79	88
107. Switzerland	-	-	-	-	99	-	-
108. Syrian Arab Rep.	76	43	99	95	67	72	49

(Contd.) Table II.3

Table II.3 (Contd.)

1	2		3		4	5	
109. Tanzania U. Rep. of	93	88 (1986)	51	53	76	04	03
110. Thailand	94	88	-	-	64	35	35
111. Togo	53	28	88	58	43	32	10
112. Trinidad and Tobago	97	95	89	92	78	74	79
113. Tunisia	68	41	99	90	78	45	33
114. Turkey	86	62 (1984)	-	-	85	56	33
115. Uganda	70	45	43 (1982)	38	58 (1978)	11 (1983)	05
116. USSR	-	-	-	-	-	-	-
117. United Arab Emirates	58 (1975)	38	87	89	97	54	66
118. United Kingdom	-	-	97	97	-	83	87
119. USA	-	-	97	97	-	100	100
120. Uruguay	93 (1975)	94	-	-	88	-	-
121. Venezuela	88	85	-	-	68 (1978)	41	50
122. Vietnam	88	80	-	-	50	44	41
123. Yemen	27	03	-	-	15	26	03
124. Yemen Dem.	59	25	-	-	40	26	11
125. Yugoslavia	97	86	-	-	98	84	80
126. Zaire	79	45	86 (1983)	65	65 (1976)	81	33
127. Zambia	84	67	-	-	85	24	14
128. Zimbabwe	81	67	-	-	79	55	37

II.4. HEALTH AND NUTRITION DATA

Country	% of Infants with Low Birth Weight (1982-87)	Average Index of Food Production per Capita (1979-81 = 100) 1986	Daily Per Capita Calorie Supply as % of Requirements 1985	% of House hold Income spent on Food 1980-85
1	2	3	4	5
1. Afghanistan	19	92	92	-
2. Albania	07	95	118	-
3. Algeria	09	104	121	-
4. Angola	17	87	86	-
5. Argentina	06	99	122	35
6. Australia	06	100	114	13
7. Austria	06	104	130	16
8. Bangladesh	31	100	78	-
9. Belgium	05	104	139	15
10. Benin	10	116	94	37
11. Bhutan	-	102	-	-
12. Bolivia	15	89	88	33
13. Botswana	08	78	95	35
14. Brazil	08	104	107	35
15. Bulgaria	06	104	146	-
16. Burkina Faso	18	126	87	-
17. Burma	16	127	117	-
18. Burundi	14	97	93	-

(Contd.) Table II.4)

Table II.4 (Contd.)

1	2	3	4	5
19. Cameroon	13	95	89	26
20. Canada	06	116	130	11
21. Central African Republic	15	94	92	-
22. Chad	11	106	79	-
23. Chile	07	106	102	29
24. China	06	125	111	-
25. Colombia	15	97	111	29
26. Congo	12	93	108	31
27. Costa Rica	09	93	118	33
28. Cote d' Ivoire	14	98	102	38
28A. Cuba	08	108	127	-
29. Czechoslovakia	06	117	143	-
30. Denmark	06	126	129	13
31. Dominican Rep.	16	97	110	46
32. Ecuador	10	101	88	31
33. Egypt	07	104	127	36
34. El Salvador	15	84	91	33
35. Ethiopia	-	88	94	32
36. Poland	04	108	111	16
37.France	05	105	142	16
38. Gabon	16	97	124	-
39. German Dem. Rep.	06	109	143	-
40. Germany Fed. Rep.	05	116	133	12

(Contd.) Table II.4

Table II.4 (Contd.)

1	2	3	4	5
41. Ghana	17	114	78	50
42. Greece	06	96	145	30
43. Guatemala	10	95	99	36
44. Guinea	18	94	85	-
45. Guinea-Bissau	20	131	105	-
46. Guyana	11	81	111	-
47. Haiti	17 (1978)	94	97	-
48. Honduras	20	90	95	39
49. Hong Kong (colony)	04	143	119	19
50. Hungary	10	110	135	25
51. **India**	30	111	94	52
52. Indonesia	14	119	109	48
53. Iran, Islamic Rep. of	09	98	118	-
54. Iraq	09	119	118	-
55. Ireland	04	99	140	22
56. Israel	07	103	119	16
57. Italy	07	100	143	19
58. Jamaica	08	93	118	33
59. Japan	05	107	106	19
60. Jordan	07	102	117	36
61. Kampuchea	-	142	85	-
62. Kenya	13	93	87	42
63. Korea, Dem. Rep. of	-	106	126	-
64. Korea Rep. of	09	107	117	35
65. Kuwait	07	—	—	—

(Contd.) Table II.4

Table II.4 (Contd.)

1	2	3	4	5
66. Lao People's Dem. Rep.	39	129	96	-
67. Lebanon	10	127	101	-
68. Lesotho	10	79	100	-
69. Liberia	-	97	103	-
70. Libyan Arab Jamahiriya	05	141	152	-
71. Madagascar	10	96	111	58
72. Malawi	10	88	96	55
73. Malaysia	09	113	110	30
74. Mali	17	103	69	57
75. Mauritius	09	107	118	20
76. Mexico	15	97	126	35
77. Mangolia	10	96	117	36
78. Morocco	09	118	108	48
79. Mozambique	15	85	68	-
80. Nepal	-	97	88	-
81. Netherlands	04	108	128	13
82. New Zealand	05	105	131	12
83. Nicaragua	15	74	105	-
84. Niger	20	91	97	-
85. Nigeria	25	105	92	52
86. Norway	04	103	114	05
87. Oman	14	-	-	-

(Contd.) Table II.4)

Table II.4 (Contd.)

1	2	3	4	5
88. Pakistan	25	104	93	54
89. Panama	08	93	98	38
90. Papua New Guinea	25	98	79	-
91. Paraguay	06	97	127	30
92. Peru	09	96	84	35
93. Philippines	18	95	101	47
94. Poland	08	110	126	29
95. Portugal	08	101	124	34
96. Romania	06	121	127	-
97. Rowanda	17	87	87	29
98. Saudi Arabia	06	202	132	-
99. Senegal	10	100	109	53
100. Sierra Leone	14	101	85	47
101. Singapore	07	90	114	19
102. Somalia	-	91	91	-
103. South Africa	12	86	118	-
104. Spain	-	101	130	24
105. Sri Lanka	28	91	114	48
106. Sudan	15	104	93	58
107. Sweden	04	103	114	13
108. Switzerland	05	105	126	17
109. Syrian Arab Rep.	09	99	129	-

(Contd.) Table II.4

Table II.4 (Contd.)

1	2	3	4	5
110. Tanzania U. Rep. of	14	92	99	62
111. Thailand	12	105	102	34
112. Togo	20	84	97	-
113. Trinidad and Tobago	-	94	126	-
114. Tunisia	07	106	119	42
115. Turkey	07	103	125	40
116. Uganda	10	129	109	-
117. USSR	06	111	128	-
118. United Arab Emirates	-	-	-	-
119. United Kingdom	07	111	129	12
120. USA	07	98	140	13
121. Uruguay	08	98	103	31
122. Venezuela	09	93	95	38
123. Vietnam	18	119	97	-
124. Yemen	09	119	93	-
125. Yemen Dem.	13	83	93	-
126. Yugoslavia	07	98	134	27
127. Zaire	-	98	96	55
128. Zambia	14	96	85	50
129. Zimbabwe	15	100	84	43

11.5 DATA ON DIVERSE ISSUES
(i) Children and Women

	Under 5 Mortality Rate 1987	Infant Mortality Rate (under I) 1987	(%) Contraceptive Prevalence 1981-85	% Pregnant Women immunized against Tetanes 1986-87	Adult Literacy Rate as percentage of Males 1985
1	2	3	4	5	6
1. Afghanistan	304	173	02 (1971-72)	06	20.5
2. Albania	48	40	65	61	-
3. Algeria	111	75	07	-	58.7
4. Angola	288	169	01	52	-
5. Argentia	38	32	74	-	99.0
6. Australia	10	09	67 (1970)	-	-
7. Austria	12	37	71	-	-
8. Bangladesh	191	120	25	07	51.2
9. Belgium	13	10	81	100	-
10. Benin	188	111	20	09	43.2
11. Bhutan	200	129	-	10	-
12. Bolivia	176	111	26	02 (1985)	77.4
13. Botswana	95	68	29	40	94.5
14. Brazil	87	64	65	-	-
15. Bulgaria	20	15	76 (1976)	-	-
16. Bukina Fasco	237	139	01	26	28.6
17. Burma	98	71	05	24	-
18. Burundi	192	113	01	59 (Hospital Data Only)	60.5

(Contd.) Table II.5(i)

Table II.5(i) (Contd.)

1	2	3	4	5	6
19. Cameroon	156	95	03 (1978	26 (1975)	0.9
20. Canada	09	08	-	73	-
21. Central African Republic	226	133	-	20 (1985)	54.7
22. Chad	227	133	01	09	27.5
23. Chile	26	20	43	-	99.0
24. China	45	33	74	-	68.3
25. Colombia	69	46	51	40 (1978)	97.8
26. Congo	117	74	-	67	77.5
27. Costa Rice	23	18	68	90	98.9
28. Cote d' Ivoire	145	97	03	68	858.5
29. Cuba	19	15	60	-	100
30. Czechoslovakia	17	13	-	-	-
31. Denmark	11	08	63 (1975)	-	-
32. Dominican Republic	84	66	47	87	98.7
33. Ecuador	89	64	40	05	94.1
34. Egypt	129	87	30	12	50.8
35. El. Salvador	87	60	47	19 (1985)	92.0
36. Ethiopia	261	105	02	05	-
37. Finland	07	06	80 (1977)	-	-
38. France	10	08	79 (1978)	-	-
39. Gabon	172	104	32	92 (1985)	75.7
40. German Dem. Rep.	12	09	-	-	-
41. Germany Fed. Rep.	11	09	-	-	-
42. Greece	17	12	-	-	90.7
43. Guatemala	103	60	01	05	47.6
44. Guinea	252	148	01	05	42.5
45. Guinea-Bissau	227	133	01	23	37.0

(Contd.) Table II.5(i)

Table II.5(i) (Contd.)

1	2	3	4	5	6
46. **Guyana**	39	31	35 (1975)	57 (1984)	97.9
47. **Haiti**	174	118	07	56 (1985)	87.5
48. **Honduras**	111	70	35	25 (1985)	95.1
49. **Hong Kong (Colony)**	10	08	73	90	85.3
50. **Hungary**	19	17	74 (979-80)	99	-
51. **India**	152	100	34	47	50.9
52. **Indonesia**	120	85	40	33	78.3
53. **Iran, Islamic Rep. of**	94	65	23	12	62.9
54. **Iraq**	96	70	14	53	96.7
55. **Ireland**	11	09	60 (1970)	-	-
56. **Isreal**	13	11	-	-	95.9
57. **Italy**	12	10	78 (1979)	-	98.0
58. **Jamaica**	23	18	50	52 (1985)	-
59. **Japan**	08	05	57	-	-
60. **Jordan**	60	45	26	28	72.4
61. **Kampuchea**	208	133	0	03	72.5
62. Kenya	116	73	17	37	70.0
63. Korea, Dem. Rep. of	34	26	-	-	-
64. Korea	34	26	-	-	91.7
65. Kuwait	23	19	-	02	82.9
66. Leo People's Dem. Rep.	163	111	-	19	82.6
67. Lebanon	53	41	53 (1971)	-	80.2
68. Lesotho	139	101	05	00	135.5
69. Liberia	150	88	01	20	48.9
70. Libyan Arab Jamahiriya	123	84	-	12	61.7
71. Madagascar	187	121	-	05	83.8

(Contd.) Table II.5(i)

Table II.5(i) (Contd.)

1	2	3	4	5	6
72. Malawi	267	151	01	20	59.6
73. Malaysia	33	24	51	25	81.5
74. Mali	296	170	01	09	47.8
75. Mauritius	30	24	75	68	86.5
76. Mexico	70	48	48	-	95.7
77. Mongolia	61	46	-	-	92.5
78. Morocco	123	84	27	33	48.9
79. Mozambique	295	170	-	59	40.0
80. Nepal	200	129	15	15	30.8
81. Netherlands	09	08	78	-	-
82. New Zealand	13	11	-	-	-
83. Nicaragua	99	63	09	25	-
84. Niger	232	126	01	05	47.4
85. Nigeria	177	106	05	12	57.4
86. Norway	08	07	71 (1977-78)	-	-
87. Oman	-	-	-	70	25.5
88. Pakistan	169	110	08	27	47.5
89. Panama	35	23	59	27	89.9
90. Papua New Guinea	85	61	04	23	63.6
91. Paraguay	63	42	39	58	93.4
92. Peru	126	89	43	06	85.7
93. Philippines	75	46	33	49	98.8
94. Poland	19	18	75 (1977)	-	-
95. Portugal	19	18	70 (1985)	-	89.9
96. Romania	28	22 (1978)	55	-	-
97. Rowanda	209	123	10	32	54.1
98. Saudi Arabia	102	72	-	50	43.7
99. Senegal	220	129	04 (1978)	08 (1985)	51.4

(Contd.) Table II.5(i)

Table II.5(i) (Contd.)

1	2	3	4	5	6
100. Sierea Leone	270	105	04	59	55.3
101. Singapore	12	09	74	90 (1985)	84.9
102. Somalia	225	133	-	06	33.3
103. South Africa	98	73	48	-	-
104. Spain	11	09	51 (1977)	-	94.8
105. Sri Lanka	45	34	57	39	91.2
106. Sudan	184	109	05 (1978-79)	12	42.4
107. Sweden	07	06	-	78	-
108. Switzerland	08	07	70 (1980)	-	-
109. Syrian Arab Rep.	67	49	20	06	56.6
110. Tanzania U. Rep. of	179	107	01	60	94.6
111. Thailand	51	40	65	61	-
112. Togo	156	95	-	64	52.8
113. Trinidad and Tobago	24	20	55	60	97.9
114. Tunisia	86	60	42 (1977)	27 (1984)	60.3
115. Turkey	97	78	38 (1978)	07	72.1
116. Uganda	172	104	01	13	64.3
117. USSR	30	25	-	-	-
118. United Arab Emirates	33	27	-	-	65.5
119. United Kingdom	11	09	83	-	-
120. U.S.A.	13	10	88	-	-
121. Uruguay	32	27	-	13 (1984)	101.8
122. Venezuela	45	36	49 (1977)	-	96.6
123. Vietnam	91	55	20	-	90.9
124. Yemen	195	117	01 (1979)	02	11.1
125. Yemen Dem.	202	112	-	08	42.4
126. Yogoslavia	28	25	55 (1976)	-	88.7
127. Zaire	164	99	01	26	57.0
128. Zambia	130	81	01	41	79.8
129. Zimbabwe	116	73	40	48	82.7

II.5(ii)Countries with Less Population

	Under 5 Mortality Rate		Intant Mortality Rate (under 1)		Total Population (millions)	Annual no of births/infant and child deaths (0-4) (thousands)	GNP Per Capita US $	Life Expectancy at Birth (years)	% Adults Literate male/female	% of age Group Enrolled in Primary School male/female
	1960	1987	1960	1987	1987	1987	1986	1987	1985	1984-1986
1. Gambia	375	264	213	153	0.8	39/10	230	44	36/15	92/58
2. Equatorial Guinea	315	217	188	128	0.4	18/4	180	47	00/00	00/00
3. Djibouti	-	-	-	123	0.4	19/2	480	48	15/9	00/00
4. Swaziland	227	177	152	119	0.7	36/6	690	57	70/66	110/108
5. Vanuatu	-	-	-	101	0.2	—	-	-	57/48	00/00
6. Comoros	216	132	128	81	0.4	23/3	320	53	56/40	90/70
7. Cape Verde	213	94	143	67	0.3	15/1	460	62	61/39	112/105
8. Sao Tome & Principe	-	91	-	74	0.1	00/00	340	-	73/42	00/00
9. Maldives	-	91	-	68	0.2	00/00	310	-	83/82	00/00
10. Solomon Islands	-	-	-	44	0.3	00/00	530	-	00/00	00/00

(Contd.) Table II.5(ii)

Table II.5(ii) (Contd.)

11. St. Christopher/Nevis	-	-	-	41	(.)	00/00	1700	65	00/00	00/00
12. Dominica	-	-	-	40	0.1	00/00	1210	77	00/00	00/00
13. Samoa	-	-	-	33	0.2	00/00	680	-	0/00	00/00
14. Saint Vincent	-	-	-	33	0.1	00/00	960	-	00/00	00/00
15. Qatar	239	43	145	32	0.3	11/(.)	13200	70	51/51	121/121
16. Suriname	96	40	70	32	0.4	10/(.)	2510	70	90/90	136/130
17. Fiji	98	33	71	27	0.7	19/1	1810	71	90/81	129/128
18. Bahrain	208	32	130	27	0.5	14(.)	8510	71	79/64	111/110
19. Bahamas	-	-	-	23	0.2	00/00	7190	-	00/00	00/00
20. Belize	-	-	-	23	0.2	00/00	1170	--	00/00	00/00
21. Antigua and Barbuda	-	-	26	21	0.1	00/00	2380	70	00/00	00/00
22. Saint Lucia	-	-	-	18	0.1	00/00	1320	73	00/00	00/00
23. Seychelles	-	21	-	17	0.1	00/00	-	70	56/60	103/102
24. Grenada	-	-	-	14	0.1	00/00	1240	66	00/00	00/00
25. Brunei Darussalam	-	-	-	12	0.2	00/00	15400	-	85/69	00/00
26. Barbados	66	15	54	11	0.3	51/(.)	5150	74	00/00	113/108
27. Cyprus	36	14	30	12	0.7	13(.)	4360	76	96/83	99/100
28. Luxembourg	41	12	33	9	0.4	4/(.)	15770	75	00/00	101/99
29. Malta	42	9	37	7	0.3	7/(.)	3450	73	86/82	99/95
30. Iceland	22	5	17	4	0.2	4/(.)	13410	78	00/00	98/110

(*Source: The State of the World's Children, 1989*)

II.5(iii) UNDP Resources

UNDP's resources are allocated to countries on the basis of need according to an internationally agreed formula. The indicative planning figure, or IPF, is the projected amount that will be available for programme activities in a country over a five-year period. The calculations are made on the basis of population, per capita gross national product (GNP), and additional criteria which weigh in favour of countries facing the greatest geographic disadvantages, such as landlocked countries, or economic difficulties, such as high debt service costs and deteriorating terms of trade.

(US $ Millions)

Countries and Territories	First Cycle 1972-1976	Second Cycle 1977-1981	Third Cycle 1982-1986	Fourth Cycle 1987-1991
AFRICA				
Angola	3.000	10.950	22.825	22.825
Benin	7.500	16.250	18.425	24.727
Botswana	5.800	8.500	4.675	4.883
Burkina Faso	10.700	23.750	30.250	39.667
Burundi	10.000	18.750	26.675	28.627
Cameroon	15.000	17.250	15.125	15.125
Cape Verde	1.500	4.000	6.188	6.188
Central African Republic	7.500	11.750	16.225	20.999
Chad	7.500	19.000	28.600	36.262
Comoros	.672	7.200	6.600	6.783
Congo	7.500	7.500	6.050	6.050
Cote d'Iroive	15.000	15.000	9.075	15.996
Equatorial Guniea	3.500	4.258	7.013	8.782
Ethiopia	20.000	42.000	61.600	77.443
Gabon	7.500	7.500	3.300	2.640
Gambia	2.500	7.000	7.838	11.476
Ghana	15.000	19.000	22.000	31.261
Guinea	15.000	21.750	24.475	28.150
Guinea-Bissau	2.500	6.120	11.962	16.414
Kenya	15.000	27.500	28.600	34.585
Lesotho	8.300	13.250	12.238	12.943
Liberia	10.000	10.000	7.425	11.567
Madagascar	10.000	23.750	26.950	34.535

Contd.) Table II.5 (iii)

Table II.5 (iii) (Contd.)

Countries and Territories	First Cycle 1972-1976	Second Cycle 1977-1981	Third Cycle 1982-1986	Fourth Cycle 1987-1991
Malawi	7.500	19.750	29.150	38.817
Mali	10.000	24.000	35.750	43.197
Mauritania	5.000	9.750	13.475	13.475
Mauritius	5.000	5.250	3.850	3.850
Mozambique	4.500	19.000	40.700	47.059
Namibia	1.000	7.750	4.263	9.395
Niger	10.000	19.750	24.750	33.958
Nigeria	30.000	45.500	30.250	30.637
Rwanda	10.000	19.750	24.750	31.367
Sao Tome & Principe	.500	1.500	1.200	2.867
Senegal	10.000	11.750	18.150	24.537
Seychelles	.751	1.600	1.200	1.200
Sierra Leone	7.500	13.250	19.195	20.814
Swaziland	5.700	5.750	3.162	3.875
Togo	10.000	11.000	12.953	21.085
Uganda	10.000	30.000	32.725	46.244
United Republic of Tanzania	15.000	33.500	39.600	51.896
Zaire	20.000	34.500	43.450	52.793
Zambia	15.000	15.000	11.687	17.608
Zimbabwe	-	5.600	13.337	16.158
Africa Subtotals	378.423	675.978	807.711	1,008.758
ASIA AND PACIFIC				
Afghanistan	20.000	38.000	39.325	51.415
Bangladesh	18.500	65.500	110.550	117.036
Bhutan	2.500	12.250	20.075	21.918
Brunei	.049	.200	.584	.467
Burma	15.000	41.500	56.100	70.684
China	-	15.00	78.100	138.337
Cook Islands	.688	1.400	1.120	1.120
Democratic Kampuchea	10.000	25.500	14.025	14.025
Democratic People's Republic of Korea	-	8.850	13.612	13.612
Fiji	5.000	5.000	2.750	2.750

(Contd.) Table II.5 (iii)

Table II.5 (iii) (Contd.)

Countries and Territories	First Cycle 1972-1976	Second Cycle 1977-1981	Third Cycle 1982-1986	Fourth Cycle 1987-1991
India	50.000	97.000	138.600	138.600
Indonesia	35.000	69.500	58.300	58.300
Iran (Islamic Republic of)	20.000	20.000	11.000	8.800
Kiribati	.500	1.140	1.040	1.778
Lao People's Dem. Rep.	5.000	17.750	28.875	32.321
Malaysia	15.000	15.000	8.250	8.250
Maldives	1.000	2.500	3.850	4.350
Mongolia	10.000	10.000	5.500	5.940
Nauru	-	.060	.048	.048
Nepal	15.000	32.500	53.900	57.851
Niue	.045	1.000	.800	.800
Pakistan	18.500	52.500	64.900	64.900
Papua New Guinea	5.000	8.750	7.425	9.916
Philippines	20.000	30.500	25.300	25.300
Republic of Korea	15.000	18.000	9.900	9.900
Samoa	5.000	5.250	2.888	3.809
Singapore	7.500	7.500	4.125	3.300
Solomon Islands	1.000	3.145	2.200	3.168
Sri Lanka	15.000	31.5000	41.800	41.800
Territory of Hong Kong	.500	.500	.275	.275
Thailand	15.000	29.500	23.650	23.650
Tokelau	-	.150	.760	1.013
Tonga	1.000	2.128	1.375	1.375
Trust Territory of Pacific Islands	-	1.000	.800	.965
Tuvalu	.005	1.140	.912	.955
Vanuatu	.588	2.000	1.200	1.612
Viet Nam	10.000	44.000	64.900	70.773
Asia and Pacific subtotals	337.375	717.213	898.814	1,001.113
LATIN AMERICA AND CARIBBEAN				
Anguilla	-	-	.640	.902
Antigua and Barbuda	.985	1.765	1.200	1.200
Argentina	20.000	20.000	11.000	11.000
Aruba	-	-	.455	.364
Bahamas	2.184	2.400	1.320	1.320

(Contd.) Table II.5 (iii)

Table II.5 (iii) (Contd.)

Countries and Territories	First Cycle 1972-1976	Second Cycle 1977-1981	Third Cycle 1982-1986	Fourth Cycle 1987-1991
Barbados	2.500	2.500	1.375	1.375
Belize	1.000	1.650	1.200	1.200
Bermuda	-	.700	.440	.352
Bolivia	15.000	15.500	10.725	20.021
Brazil	30.000	30.000	16.500	16.500
British Virgin Islands	.309	.300	.240	.240
Cayman Islands	.620	.700	.448	.448
Chile	20.000	20.000	11.000	11.000
Colombia	20.000	20.000	12.100	12.100
Costa Rica	5.000	5.000	2.750	4.571
Cuba	10.000	13.500	11.275	11.275
Dominica	.704	1.362	1.265	1.265
Dominican Republic	7.500	7.500	6.600	6.600
Ecuador	15.000	15.000	8.250	8.250
El Salvador	5.000	9.250	8.388	9.030
Grenada	.980	1.880	1.200	1.200
Guatemala	7.500	8.000	7.150	7.150
Guyana	5.000	5.000	4.675	8.651
Haiti	6.000	18.750	20.900	29.665
Honduras	5.000	9.250	8.800	9.806
Jamaica	7.500	7.500	4.125	4.125
Mexico	20.000	20.000	11.000	11.000
Montserrat	.283	.400	.560	.560
Netherlands Antilles	1.837	1.900	.745	.596
Nicaragua	5.000	5.323	5.225	7.827
Panama	7.500	7.500	4.125	4.125
Paraguay	7.500	7.500	5.362	5.362
Peru	15.000	15.000	13.750	13.750
Saint Christopher & Nevis	.690	.700	1.200	1.200
Saint Helena			.264	.440
Saint Lucia	.902	1.765	1.200	1.200
Saint Vincent and the Grenadines	.685	1.420	1.788	1.788
Suriname	2.500	3.500	1.925	1.925
Trinidad and Tobago	5.000	5.000	2.750	2.200
Turks and Caicos Islands	.332	.400	.680	.822

(Contd.) Table II.5 (iii)

Table II.5 (iii) (Contd.)

Countries and Territories	First Cycle 1972-1976	Second Cycle 1977-1981	Third Cycle 1982-1986	Fourth Cycle 1987-1991
Uruguay	10.000	10.000	5.500	5.500
Venezuela	10.000	10.000	5.500	4.400
Latin America and Caribbean subtoals	275.011	307.915	215.595	242.305
ARAB STATES AND EUROPE				
Albania	1.000	4.250	5.638	5.638
Algeria	20.000	20.000	11.000	11.000
Bahrain	2.500	2.500	1.375	1.100
Bulgaria	7.500	7.500	3.300	3.300
Cyprus	5.000	5.000	2.750	2.750
Czechoslovakia	2.500	2.500	1.375	—
Democratic Yemen	10.000	14.500	12.238	13.058
Djibouti	-	2.200	2.887	2.887
Egypt	27.500	31.500	30.800	33.494
Greece	7.500	7.500	3.300	—
Hungary	7.500	3.500	1.925	1.925
Iceland	1.000	-	-	-
Iraq	15.000	15.000	8.250	8.250
Israel	5.000	-	-	-
Jordan	15.000	15.000	8.250	8.250
Kuwait	1.000	-	-	-
Lebanon	10.000	10.000	5.500	5.500
Libyan Arab Jamahiriya	5.000	5.000	2.750	2.200
Malta	2.500	2.500	1.375	1.375
Morocco	20.000	20.000	14.850	19.001
Oman	4.000	4.000	2.200	1.760
Poland	7.500	7.500	3.200	4.125
Portugal	-	4.000	2.200	2.200
Qatar	1.500	-	-	.660
Romania	7.500	7.500	4.125	4.125
Saudi Arabia	10.000	10.000	5.500	4.400
Somalia	15.000	18.250	26.400	30.050
Spain	5.000	-	-	-
Sudan	20.000	33.000	32.175	39.774
Syrian Arab Republic	15.000	15.000	8.250	8.250

(Contd.) Table II.5 (iii)

Table II.5 (iii) (Contd.)

Countries and Territories	First Cycle 1972-1976	Second Cycle 1977-1981	Third Cycle 1982-1986	Fourth Cycle 1987-1991
Tunisia	15.000	15.000	8.250	8.250
Turkey	20.000	20.000	11.000	11.000
United Arab Emirates	1.000	1.000	.550	.550
Yemen	15.000	23.750	16.500	23.165
Yugoslavia	7.500	7.500	4.125	4.125
Arab States and Europe Subtotals	309.500	334.950	242.138	262.162
Country IPF totals:	1,300.309	2,036.056	2,164.258	2,524.339
Africa Regional	71.200	109.400	155.870	195.750
Asia and Pacific Regional	40.700	95.700	162.855	182.720
Arab States & Europe Regional	19.700	44.300	40.700	49.820
Latin American and Caribbean Regional	61.500	63.000	42.075	49.700
Regional IPF Totals:	193.100	312.400	401.500	477.990
Interregional IPF	22.400	33.600	40.425	48.000
Global IPF	15.500	50.200	63.140	75.000
National Liberattion Movements -	20.500	8.250	10.200	
Caribbean Multi-Island	4.489	7.000	2.484	2.500
Unallocated	6.191	2.610	-	27.531
GRAND TOTALS:	1,541.990	2,462.370	2,680.060	3,165.560

Source: (UNDP World Development Annual Report 1987)

II.5(iv) IBRD and IDA Projects - 1988

Assistance in Fiscal Year 1988, by Region

(amounts in millions of US dollars)

	IBRD loans		IDA credits		Total	
Region and Country	Number	Amount	Number	Amount	Number	Amount
Africa						
Benin	-	-	1	21.0	1	21.0
Burkina Faso	-	-	1	17.9	1	17.9
Burundi	-	-	5	153.5	5	153.5
Cameroon	1	103.0	-	-	1	103.0
Cape Verde	-	-	1	4.2	1	4.2
Central African Rep.	-	-	3	73.0	3	73.0
Chad	-	-	3	78.4	3	78.4
Congo, People's Republic of the	2	85.2	-	-	2	85.2
Cote d'Ivoire	1	57.4	-	-	1	57.4
Ethiopia	-	-	2	103.0	2	103.0
Gabon	1	50.0	-	-	1	50.0
Ghana	-	-	6	261.1	6	261.1
Guinea	-	-	4	148.7	4	148.7
Guinea-Bissau	-	-	2	14.0	2	14.0
Kenya	-	-	3	133.8	3	133.8
Lesotho	-	-	2	36.4	2	36.4
Madagascar	-	-	4	180.5	4	180.5
Malawi	-	-	3	89.3	3	89.3
Mali	-	-	3	89.3	3	89.3
Mauritania	-	-	1	10.0	1	10.0
Mauritius	1	10.0	-	-	1	10.0
Mozambique	-	-	2	85.9	2	85.9
Niger	-	-	3	46.3	3	46.3
Nigeria	3	342.8	-	-	3	342.8
Senegal	-	-	4	129.6	4	129.6
Somalia	-	-	2	18.0	2	18.0
Sudan	-	-	3	139.7	3	139.7
Tanzania	-	-	1	60.0	1	60.0
Togo	-	-	4	111.6	4	111.6
Uganda	-	-	4	142.4	4	142.4
Zaire	-	-	2	56.0	2	56.0
Zimbabwe	2	76.7	-	-	2	76.7
Total	11	725.1	69	2,203.6	80	2,928.7

(Contd.) Table II.5 (iv)

Table II.5 (iv) (Contd.)

Region and Country	IBRD loans		IDA credits		Total	
	Number	Amount	Number	Amount	Number	Amount
Asia						
Bangladesh	-	-	5	227.8	5	227.8
Bhutan	-	-	2	5.3	2	5.3
Burma	-	-	1	63.0	1	63.0
China	10	1,053.7	4	639.9	14	1,693.6
Fiji	1	23.4	-	-	1	23.4
India	8	2,255.0	2	717.2	10	2,972.2
Indonesia	10	1,375.3	-	-	10	1,375.3
Korea, Republic of	3	196.0	-	-	3	196.0
Lao People's Democratic Republic	-	-	1	14.1	1	14.1
Malaysia	3	170.2	-	-	3	170.2
Nepal	-	-	3	71.2	3	71.2
Philippines	4	505.0	-	-	4	505.0
Sri Lanka	-	-	5	179.5	5	179.5
Thailand	3	173.0	-	-	3	173.0
Total	42	5,751.6	23	1,918.0	65	7,669.6
Europe, Middle East, and North Africa						
Algeria	4	391.0	-	-	4	391.0
Cyprus	2	65.0	-	-	2	65.0
Hungary	3	320.0	-	-	3	320.0
Jordan	3	107.0	-	-	3	107.0
Morocco	3	338.0	-	-	3	338.0
Pakistan	3	277.4	2	189.5	5	466.9
Portugal	2	92.0	-	-	2	92.0
Tunisia	5	291.0	-	-	5	291.0
Turkey	4	1,063.9	-	-	4	1,063.9
Yemen Arab Republic	-	-	2	35.6	2	35.6
Yugolsavia	2	188.0	-	-	2	188.0
Total	31	3,133.3	4	225.1	35	3,358.4

(Contd.) Table II.5 (iv)

Table II.5 (iv) (Contd.)

	IBRD loans		IDA credits		Total	
Region and Country	Number	Amount	Number	Amount	Number	Amount
Latin America and the Caribbean						
Argentina	3	626.5	-	-	3	626.5
Belize	2	13.4	-	-	2	13.4
Bolivia	-	-	3	112.0	3	112.0
Brazil	9	1,359.5	-	-	9	1,359.5
Chile	1	250.0	-	-	1	250.0
Colombia	3	465.0	-	-	3	465.0
Dominican Republic	1	105.0	-	-	1	105.0
Ecuador	2	160.0	-	-	2	160.0
El Salvador	1	65.0	-	-	1	65.0
Guatemala	1	29.0	-	-	1	29.0
Jamaica	2	26.3	-	-	2	26.3
Mexico	8	2,030.0	-	-	8	2,030.0
Uruguay	1	22.3	-	-	1	22.3
Total	34	5,152.0	3	112.0	37	5,264.0
Grand Total	11814,762.0	99	4,458.7	217	19,220.7	

Note: Supplements, as well as B-loans, are included in the amounts, but are not counted as separate lending operations. Joint IBRD/IDA operations are counted only once, as IBRD operations.

(*Source: The World Bank: Annual Report, 1988*)

INDIA IN 1988

CHAPTER 3

LAND AND ITS PEOPLE

India that is Bharat covering a land area of 32,87,232 sq. kms is the seventh largest and the second most populous country of the world. It stretches 3,214 km from North to South between the extreme latitudes and 2,933 km from East to West between the extreme longitudes. On this 2.4 per cent of earth's surface live 15 per cent (80 crore people) of world's population.

Fig. III.1: Population in India 1951 to 1988

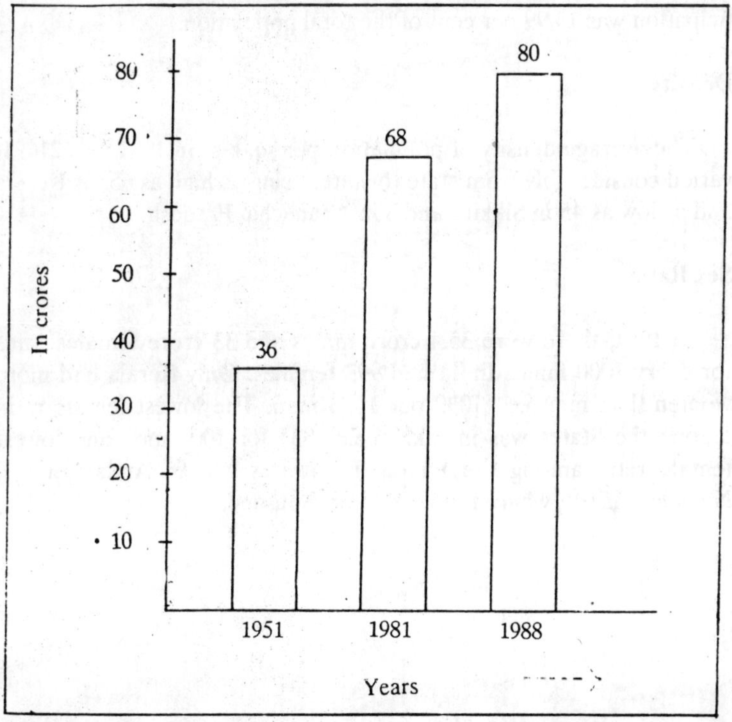

Population

Over 160 million people are added annually to our population. (President's Republic Day Speech, 25th Jan. 1989). Since 1881, the census in India has been taken regularly every ten years. According to the 1981 census, the total population of India (including the projected population of Assam) was 68,51,84,692. As compared to the 1971 census, it showed an increase of 25 per cent. 525 million person accounting for 76.7 per cent of the total Indian population lived in villages. The proportion of urban population to total population was 23.3 per cent.

In 1988, India's urban population was around 160 million which gave us the fourth largest urban population in the world. Almost 27 per cent of our urban is concentrated in 12 major cities.

The population of the main workers, who had worked for the major part of the year, to total population was 33.45 per cent. The male workers accounted for 51.62 per cent while female work participation was 13.99 per cent of the total population.

Density

The average density of population per sq. km. in 1981 was 216. It varied considerably from state to state, being as high as 655 is Kerala and as low as 45 in Sikkim and 8 in Arunachal Pradesh.

Sex Ratio

In 1981, there were 35.4 crore males and 33 crore females; thus for every 1000 males India had 993 females. Only Kerala had more women than man i.e., 1032 per 1000 men. The lowest female ratio among the States was in Sikkim i.e. 835 for 1000 men and lowest female ratio among the Union Territories was in Andaman and Nicobar Islands, where it was 760 per thousand.

Area, Population, Density and Capitals of States and Union Territories 1981

INDIA/State/ Union Territory	Area in sq. km. (000)	Population	Density of Population per sq. km.	State Capital
INDIA[1]	3,287.3[2]	68,51,84,692	216[3]	
1. Andhra Pradesh	275.1[5]	5,35,49,673	195	Hyderabad
2. Arunachal Pradesh	83.7[5]	6,31,839	8	Itanagar
3. Assam[4]	78.4	1,98,96,843	254	Dispur
4. Bihar	173.9[5]	6,99,14,734	402	Patna
5. Goa	3.7	10,07,749	N.A.	Panaji
6. Gujarat	196.0[5]	3,40,85,799	174	Gandhinagar
7. Haryana	44.2[5]	1,29,22,618	292	Chandigarh
8. Himachal Pradesh	55.7	42,80,818	77	Shimla
9. Jammu & Kashmir	222.2[5]	59,87,389	59[3]	Sri Nagar
10. Karnataka	191.8	3,71,35,714	194	Bangalore
11. Kerala	38.9[5]	2,54,53,680	655	Trivandrum
12. Madhya Pradesh	443.4[5]	5,21,78,844	118	Bhopal
13. Maharashtra	307.7[5]	6,27,84,171	204	Bombay
14. Manipur	22.3	14,20,953	64	Imphal
15. Meghalaya	22.4[5]	13,35,819	60	Shillong
16. Mizoram	21.1	4,93,757	23	Aizawal
17. Nagaland	16.6	7,74,930	47	Kohima
18. Orissa	155.7	2,63,70,271	169	Bhubaneswar
19. Punjab	50.4	1,67,88,915	333	Chandigarh
20. Rajasthan	342.2	3,42,61,862	100	Jaipur
21. Sikkim	7.1	3,16,385	45	Gangtok
22. Tamil Nadu	130.1[5]	4,84,08,077	372	Madras
23. Tripura	10.5	20,53,058	196	Agartala
24. Uttar Pradesh	294.4[5]	11,08,62,013	377	Lucknow
25. West Bengal	88.8[5]	5,45,80,647	615	Calcutta
1. Andaman and Nicobar Islands	8.3	1,88,741	23	Port Blair
2. Chandigarh	0.1	4,51,610	3,961	Chandigarh
3. Dadra and Nagar Haveli	0.5	1,03,676	211	Silvassa
4. Daman and Diu	0.11	78,981	N.A.	
5. Delhi	1.5	62,20,406	4,194	Delhi
6. Lakshawdeep	.03	40,249	1,258	Kavaaratti
7. Pondicherry	0.5	6,04,4,71	1,229	Pondicherry

1. The population figure excludes population of areas under unlawful occupation of Pakistan and China where census could not be taken.
2. The total area of the country represents provisional 'Geographical Areas' as on 31 March 1982, supplied by the Survey of India. The area includes 78,114 sq. km. under illegal occupation of Pakistan, 5,180 sq. km. illegally handed over by Pakistan to China and 37,555 sq. km under illegal occupation of China in Ladakh district.
3. The density has been worked out on a comparable data.

4. Projected figures for 1981.
5. The area figures are provisional.
   N.A. = Not available.

(*Source*: India 1987).

Most Populated State	:	Uttar Pradesh
Largest Area State	:	Madhya Pradesh
Most Density Populated State	:	Kerala
Least Populated State	:	Sikkim
Smallest Area State	:	Sikkim
Least Density Populated State	:	Sikkim

Density and Population

Year	Density per sq. km.	Decade	Percentage increase in population
1921	81	—	—
1931	90	1921-31	11.0
1941	103	1931-41	14.2
1951	117	1941-51	13.3
1961	10	1951-61	21.5
1971	177[1]	1961-71	24.8
1981[2]	216[1]	1971-81	25.0

1. Density has been worked out on a comparable data.
2. 1981 figures have been worked out after including projected figures of Assam.

Literacy Rate Per 1.000 by Sex

Year	Males	Females	Persons
1901	98	6	53
1911	106	11	58
1921	122	18	72
1931	156	29	95
1941	249	73	61
1951	249	79	167
1961	344	130	240
1971	395	187	295
1981	469	248	62

(*Source: India 1987*)

Major Religious Populations and Persuations (1981) - Excluding Assam

Religious Community	Population	Percentage to Total Population
Hindus	54,97,24,717	82.63
Muslims	7,55,71,514	11.36
Christians	1,61,74,498	2.43
Sikhs	1,30,78,146	1.96
Buddhists	47,19,900	0.71
Jains	31,92,572	0.48
Other Persuations	27,66,285	0.42
Religion not State	60,217	0.01

According to 1981 census, the literacy percentage is 36.23. Out of this 46.89 per cent of males and 24.82 per cent of females were literate. According to UNESCO, these figures were 57 per cent for males and 29 for females in 1985. The table presents the literacy rates in the country. In working out these rates for 1981, the population of Assam has been excluded. The rates up to 1941 are for undivided India. Of the total population nearly 64 per cent of the people were illiterate.

Languages

The detailed data from the 1981 census which was made available only in 1988, enumerates the main languages spoken in the household and not the mother tongue and groups related languages under a dominant language. By this count, 106 languages are separately recognised. Of these 94 are spoken by 10,000 or more people.

There were 1562 mother tongues, 10 writing systems, 67 languages as used in the school system out of 200 codified languages.

Fifteen languages have been specified in the Eighth Schedule of the Constitution. These are: Assamese, Bengali, Gujarati, Hindi, Kannada, Kashmiri, Malayalam, Marathi, Oriya, Punjabi, Sanskrit, Sindhi, Tamil, Telugu and Urdu.

Demographic Data 1987

1. Population	-	80 crore (Estimated)
2. Crude Birth Rate	-	32 per 1,000
3. Crude Death Rate	-	11 per 1,000
4. Life Expectancy	-	59
5. Total Fertility Rate	-	4.2
6. Infant mortality rate under one year age	-	100 per 1000
7. Under 5 mortality Rate	-	152 per 1000
8. Annual No of Births	-	2,67,83,000
9. Annual No of Deaths (0-4)	-	40,80,000
10. Urbanised Population	-	27%
11. Population under 16	-	315.4 million
12. Population under 5	-	111.5 million
13. No. of towns in 1981	-	3949
14. No. of Villages in 1981	-	5,57,137
15. Population of Scheduled Castes in 1981	-	10,47,54,623
16. Population of Scheduled Tribes in 1981	-	5,16,28,636

National Flag

The national flag is horizontally tricolour with deep saffron *(Kesari)* at the top, white in the middle and dark green at the bottom in equal proportion. The ratio of the width of the Flag to its length is two to three. In the centre of the white band is a wheel, in navy blue, which represents the *Charkha*. Its design is that of the wheel *(Chakra)* which appears on the abacus of the Sarnath Lion Capital of Asoka. Its diameter approximates to the width of the white band and it has 24 spokes.

The design of the National Flag was adopted by the Constituent Assembly of India on 22 July 1947. Its use and display are regulated by a code.

State Emblem

The State Emblem of India is an adaptation from the Sarnath Lion Capital of Asoka as preserved in the Sarnath Museum. In the original, there are four lions, standing back to back, mounted on an abacus with a frieze carrying sculptures in high relief of an elephant, a galloping horse, a bull and a lion separated by intervening wheels *(Chakras)* over a bell-shaped lotus. Carved out of a single block of polished sandstone, the Capital is crowned by the Wheel of the Law *(Dharma Chakra)*.

In the State Emblem adopted by the Government of India on 26 January 1950, only three lions are visible, the fourth being hidden from view. The wheel appears in relief in the centre of the abacus with a bull on the right and a horse on the left and the outlines of the other wheels on the extreme right and left. The bell-shaped lotus has been omitted. The words *Satyameva Jayate* from the *Mundaka Upanishad*, meaning 'Truth alone Triumphs', are inscribed below the abacus in Devanagari script.

National Anthem

The song *Jana-gana-mana*, composed by Rabindranath Tagore (1861-1941) was adopted by the Constituent Assembly as the National Anthem of India on 24 January 1950. It was first sung on 27 December 1911 at the Calcutta Session of the Indian National Congress. The complete song consists of five stanzas. The first stanza constitutes the full version of the National Anthem. It reads:

Jana-gana-mana-adhinayaka, jaya he
Bharata-bhagya-vidhata
Punjaba-Sindhu-Gujrata-Maratha-
Dravida-Utkala-Banga
Vindhya-Himachala-Yamuna-Ganga
Uchchala-jaladhi-taranga.
Tava shubha name jage,
tava shubha asisa, mage,
gahe tava jaya-gatha,
Jana-gana-mangala-dayaka jaya he
Bharata-bhagya-vidhata.
Jaya he, jaya he, jaya he,
Jaya jaya jaya, jaya he!.

Playing time of the full version of the National Anthem is approximately 52 seconds. A short version consisting of the first and last lines of the stanza (playing time approximately 20 seconds) is also played on certain occasions. The following is Tagore's English rendering of this stanza:

Thou art the ruler of the minds of all people,
dispenser of India's destiny.
Thy name rouses the hearts of Punjab, Sind, Gujarat and
Maratha.
Of the Dravida and Orissa and Bengal;
it echoes in the hills of the Vindhyas and Himalayas,
mingles in the music of Jamuna and Ganges
and is chanted by the waves of the Indian Sea.
They pray for thy blessings and sing thy praise.
The saving of all people waits in thy hand,
thou dispenser of India's destiny.
Victory, victory, victory to thee.

National Song

The song *Vande Mataram,* composed by Bankimchandra Chatterji (1838-1894) was a source of inspiration to the people in their struggle for freedom. It has an equal status with *Jana-gana-mana.* The first political occasion on which it was sung was the 1896 session of the Indian National Congress. The following is the text of its first stanza:

Vande Mataram!
Sujalam, suphalam, malayaja shitalam,
Shasyashyamalam, Mataram!
Shubhrajyotsna pulakitayaminim,
Phullakusumita drumadala shobhinim,
Suhasinim sumadhura bhashinim,
Sukhadam, varadam, Mataram!

The English translation of the stanza rendered by Sri Aurobindo (1872-1950) in prose*[1] is:

---

1. * As published in volume 8 of Sri Aurobindo Birth Centenary Library Popular Edition 1972.

I bow to thee, Mother,
richly-watered, richly-fruited,
cool with the winds of the south,
dark with the crops of the harvests,
the Mother!
Her nights rejoicing in the glory of the moonlight,
her lands clothed beautifully with her trees in flowering bloom,
sweet of laughter, sweet of speech,
the Mother, giver of boons, giver of bliss.

National Calendar

A uniform National Calendar based on the Saka era with Chaitra as its first month and a normal year of 365 days was adopted from 22 March 1957 along with the Gregorian calendar for the following official purposes:
(i) the Gazette of India, (ii) news broadcast by All India Radio, (iii) calendars issued by the Government of India, and (iv) government communications addressed to members of the public.

The dates of the National Calendar have a permanent correspondence with the dates of the Gregorian calendar; 1 Chaitra falling on 22 March normally and on 21 March in a leap year.

National Animal

The majestic tiger *Panthera tigris* (Linnaeus), the national animal of India for its rich colour, illusive design and formidable power, has always been held in high esteem in India. Among the carnivores, the tiger is very gorgeous and attractive with roaring voice as symbol of power. Out of eight race of the species known the world over, the Indian race is the Bengal tiger. The Royal Bengal Tiger occurs throughout the country and is also found in Nepal, Bhutan and Bangladesh. As shrinkage of habitat in India dwindled its population to only 1,827 in 1972, the Project Tiger was launched on 1 April 1973. Since then there is a gradual increase in its population estimated to be 4,230 in April 1986.

National Bird

The Indian peacock *Pavo cristatus* (Linnaeus), the national bird of India, is one of the most beautiful birds, particularly the males having the glistering blue neck, breast, fanshape crest and long magnificent tail. The courtship dance of the male by fanning up the tail before the female is most spectacular. From time immemorial, this bird has found a profound place in Indian literature, folklore and legends.

The Indian peafowl, as the peacock is called, is widely distributed in the country from south and east of India. Jammu and Kashmir, east Assam, south of Mizoram and the whole of Indian Peninsula. It is fully protected under the Indian Wild Life (Protection) Act. 1972.

(Source: India 1987)

Presidents of India

1950-1962	– Rajendra Prasad
1962-1967	– S. Radhakrishnan
1967-1969	– Zakir Hussain
1969-1974	– V.V. Giri
1974-1977	– Fakhruddin Ali Ahmed
1977-1982	– N. Sanjeeva Reddy
1982-1987	– Zail Singh
1987	– R. Venkataraman

Vice-Presidents of India

1952-1962	– Dr. S. Radhakrishnan
1962-1967	– Dr. Zakir Hussain
1967-1969	– V.V. Giri
1969-1974	– G.S. Pathak
1974-1979	– B.D. Jatti
1979-1984	– M. Hidayatullah
1984-1987	– R. Venkataraman
1987	– Dr. S.D. Sharma

Prime Ministers of India

August 15, 1947 – May 27, 1964	-	Jawaharlal Nehru
May 27, 1964 – June 9, 1964	-	Gulzari Lal Nanda (Acting)
June 9, 1964 – January 11, 1966	-	Lal Bahadur Shastri
January 11, 1966 –January 24, 1966	-	Gulzari Lal Nanda (Acting)
January 24, 1966 –March 24, 1977	-	Indira Gandhi
March 24, 1977 –July 28, 1979	-	Morarji Desai
July 28, 1979 –January 14, 1980	-	Charan Singh
January 14, 1980 –October 31,1984	-	Indira Gandhi
October 31, 1984	-	Rajiv Gandhi

Speakers of the Lok Sabha

1952-1956	-	G.V. Mavlankar
1956-1962	-	Ananthasayanam Ayyangar
1962-1967	-	S. Hukam Singh
1967-1969	-	N. Sanjeeva Reddy
1969-1975	-	G.S. Dhillon
1975-1977	-	B.R. Bhagat
March 1977 July – 1977	-	N. Sanjeeva Reddy
1977-1979	-	K.S. Hegde
1980	-	Balram Jakhar

Important Days

National Youth Day	-	January 12
Army Day	-	January 15
Republic Day	-	January 26
International Customs Day	-	January 26
Martyrs' Day	-	January 30
National Science Day	-	February 28
International Women's Day	-	March 8
World Disabled Day	-	March 15
World Forestry Day	-	March 21
National Maritime Day	-	April 5
World Health Day	-	April 7
May Day (Worker's Day: International Labour Day)	-	May 1
World Red Cross Day	-	May 8

Commonwealth Day	-	May 24
World Environment Day	-	June 5
Hiroshima Day	-	August 6
Quit India Day	-	August 9
Nagasaki Day	-	August 9
Independence Day	-	August 15
Teacher's Day	-	September 5
World Literacy Day	-	September 8
World Tourism Day	-	September 27
World Habitat Day	-	October 5
Air Force Day	-	October 8
Post Office Day	-	October 19
Word Standard Day	-	October 14
World Food Day	-	October 16
UN Day	-	October 24
National Rededication Day	-	October 31
Children's Day	-	November 14
National Integration Day	-	November 19
Navy Day	-	December 4
Flag Day	-	December 7
Human Rights Day (UN)	-	December 10
Kisan's Day	-	December 23

CHAPTER 4

INDIA SINCE INDEPENDENCE

Going back, India that is Bharat was the richest and the most prosperous country in the world. It was then known as the 'Golden Sparrow'. The standard of living of the common man was reasonably high. Articles of everyday needs were available in plenty. A common man could get easily things like: milk, butter, ghee and foodgrains. Literally speaking 'Rivers of milk flowed'. Indian handicrafts and industrial products were known for their excellence of design and quality all over the world. From the richness of this land and from the labour and wisdom of its people had sprung great wealth, great ideas, great skills and arts. Naturally, therefore, foreigners were tempted to come to India for learning, as well for loot and plunder.

The well-knit economic organisation of the country received a serious setback with the advent of invaders and especially with the British rulers who were primarily concerned with the governance of the country, not its growth. They were greatly interested in draining out wealth from India. Industrial crafts, industries and agriculture, all suffered heavily. As a result, India became a poor country. People remained underfed, ill-housed, and scantily dressed.

The statement 'A rich country inhabited by the poor people' seems paradoxical and strage. But it is still true to a considerable extent though since independence we have made a spectacular progress in different fields. The giant irrigation dams at Bhakra, Hirakund and Nagarjunasagar; the huge steel mills at Bhilai, Bokaro, Rourkela, and Durgapur, the fertiliser factories at Sindri and Nangal; the 1000-tonne per day ammonia plant (said to be the largest in the world) at Tuticorn; the aircraft factories at Bangalore, Hyderabad and Nasik; the locomotive factory at Chittaranjan; the atomic reactor at Trombay; the rocket launching station at

Sriharikota; the ISRO'S establishments like Vikram Sarabhai Space Centre, Trivandrum and Space Application Centre, Ahmedabad; launching of Indian Satellite Bhaskra and Rohini; three axis-stabilised geostationary Communication Satellite; APPLE (Ariane Passenger Payload Experiment), establishment of Indian National Satellite System (INSAT); participation of an Indian Cosmonaut in a joint Indo-Soviet Space Flight; nuclear explosion at Pokaran, etc., are the prized possessions of the Indian Nation.

Militarily we are among the first five countries in the world.

India is the sixth country to successfully detonate a nuclear device as part of its successful experiment for peace purposes.

We have the third largest reservior of highly skilled scientific and technical manpower in the world.

India is the fifth nation to have its remote sensing satellite.

We have achieved self-sufficiency in foodgrains.

India is the third largest producer of books in English, next to the U.S.A. and U.K.

The problem of eradication of poverty of the masses became the first consideration of the government soon after we achieved independence. We decided to adopt the system of planned development for tackling our problem of poverty which was linked with rising prices, low production, unemployment and inequalities of income.

To frame a development plan for independent India, the Planning Commission was set up in March 1950, by a resolution of the Government of India. The aims of planning as defined by the resolution, were, "to promote a rapid rise in the standard of living of the people by efficient exploitation of the resources of the country, increasing production, and offering opportunities to all for employment in the service of the community".

The First Five Year Plan was initiated in April 1951. This covered the period 1951-1956. So far we have had Six Five Year Plans and three Yearly Plans. The Seventh Five Year Plan covers the period 1985 to 1990.

The most important achievement of planning in the post-independence period is our self-sufficiency in foodgrains. Now we need not import foodgrains for domestic requirements as we did till a few years ago. The production is expected to touch a high figure of about 172 million tonnes in 1988-89 as against 51 million tonnes in 1950-51.

As a result of many multipurpose projects, area under irrigation increased from 226 lakh hectares in 1950 to 750 lakh hectares in 1987-88.

Our industry has many strengths: a wide range of products, a demonstrable ability to absorb and operate high technology, a large entrepreneurial capability and ample managerial and technical skills.

During the Plans, industrial production has made rapid strides, both in terms of quality and quantity.

In the year 1950-51, there were only two major units producing iron and steel. Now we have six major steel plants. Steel production rose from about one million tonnes in 1950-51, to about 7.78 million tonnes in 1987-88.

Cotton textile industry holds the second place in the production of cloth in the world. At present there are about 700 textiles mills in the country.

In 1951, we had 138 sugar mills in the country. This number increased to 351 in 1987. About half the mills are in the public sector.

Over the same period the production of cement increased from 2.69 million tonnes to 36.5 million tonnes.

The generation of electric power registered a twenty-fold increase.

Public sector in the field of industries has witnessed a very significant rise. In 1951, we had only 5 public undertakings whereas there were 188 public undertakings in 1987, in the Central Sector.

By 1985, the road network in the country had become very elaborate system of national highways, state and district roads, and rural roads totalling about 18 lakh km. This was four and a half times the figure of 4 lakh km. of roads in 1950-51.

Between 1950-51 and 1984-85, the number of trucks rose from 82,000 to 7,63,000 and buses from 34,000 to 2,06,000.

Per capita income increased from Rs. 246 in 1950-51 to about Rs.3,000 in 1987-88 at current prices.

Prior to independence, average life span of an Indian was 32 years. To-day it has lengthened to 59 years.

Our Constitution can be described as a charter of freedom. It enshrines the supremacy of the will of the people and their resolve to secure for all citizens: Justice, social, economic and political; Equality of status and opportunity, and to promote among them all Fraternity assuring the dignity of the individual and the unity of the nation. The will of the people is exercised through universal adult franchise and a parliamentary democracy. Election to Parliament and State legislatures are open contests for all political parties, and independent candidates also enjoy full scope to express themselves.

Notwithstanding various problems and the magnitude of the task of conducting elections, we have eight general elections with great success. They have been hailed both for the peaceful and the fair manner in which they were conducted. Barring the period March 1977 to July 15, 1979, when the Janta Party was in power at the Centre, the Congress had held the reigns of the Government since the first General Election in 1951-52.

Many political changes accompanied by government changes especially in States have taken place in the country since independence, through peaceful and constitutional means. Transfer of power from one party to another has taken place as a natural course and in an orderly manner.

Fig. IV.1: Election Symbols
Recognised Parties

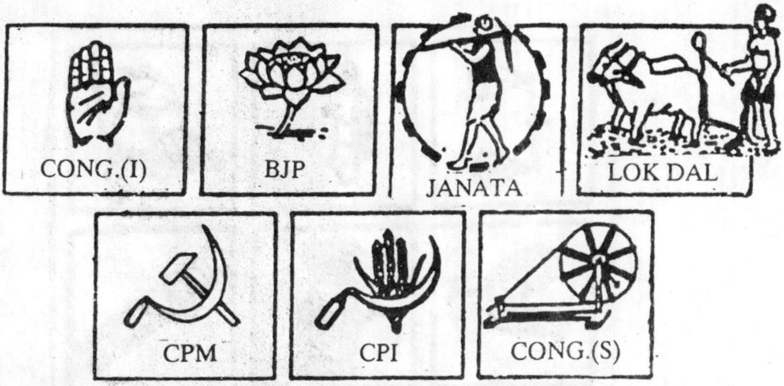

Another historic step in the development of democracy in the country was the inauguration of Panchayati Raj in October 1959. The Panchayati Raj aims at giving authority and responsibility to the village people and helping them play an active role in local development through the Panchayats. There are over 228,500 village Panchayats in the country covering practically the entire population of India.

With the Panchayati Raj, we now have parliamentary democracy in operation from the Gram Sabha to the Lok Sabha.

We have got an esablished judicial system.

Tasks Ahead

A large part of our population still remains backward. There is a wide gulf between the rich and the poor. Unemployment is on the increase. National integration is our urgent need. Erosion in the standard of values is to be checked and a crusade for 'clean life, clean politics and clean Administration' must be given first priority.

India is on the move. The tasks before as are very challenging and tremendous. But there is no cause for despair. By harnessing all our resources and working unitedly and sincerely, we can usher in an era of peace, progress and prosperity.

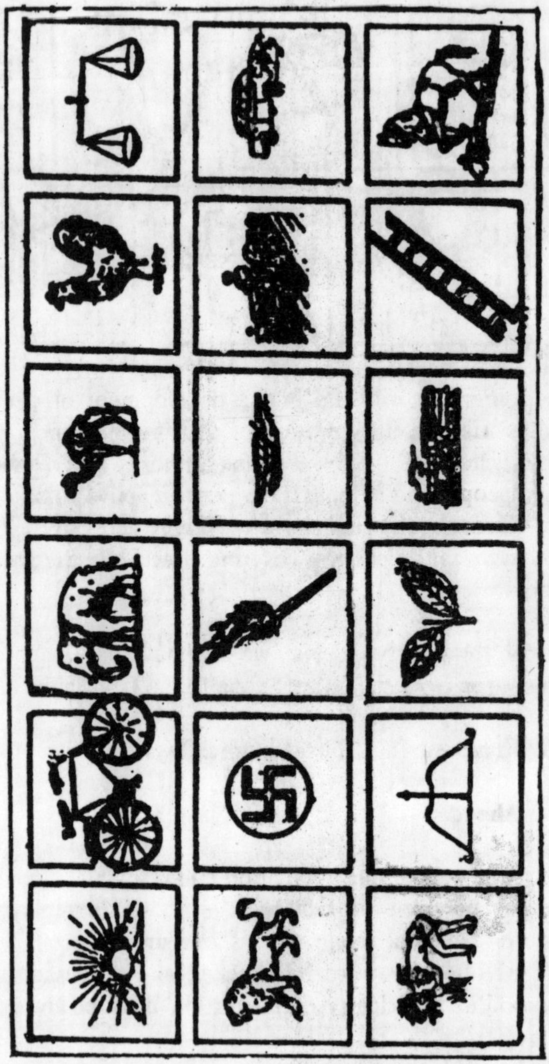

Fig. IV.2: Free Symbols for other than Recognised Parties and Independents Planning in India

The 21st century backons us holding forth new hopes. We, the people of India, must march ahead as an integrated resurgent.

Vibrant nation to meet it. As Gurudev would advise, we must "hold the faith firm", surely "the day will dawn".

CHAPTER 5

FIVE YEAR PLANS

The Planning Commission is a high powered Central Agency which was constituted in March 1950 to prepare a blue-print for development of the country. It has been entrusted with the task of assessing the resources of the country, drawing up plans for the development and utilisation of resources within the framework of specified national priorities and determining conditions, modalities and adjustments needed for the success of the planning process. The Commission also appraises the progress of the plans form time to time.

The Prime Minister is the Chairman of the Commission. In order to achieve co-ordination among the States in implementing the plans and to achieve targets set in the plans, an advisory body called National Development Council was set up in 1952, with the Prime Minister as Chairman and Chief Minister of all the States and Administrators of the Union Territories as members.

Broadly speaking the national plans are formulated and finalised in three stages. In the First stage, the rough projections and estimates, prepared by the Planning Commission in consultation with the Central Ministries and State Governments against the background of the long-term perspective, are approved and modified if necesary by the NDC in the form of preliminary instructions.

In the Second stage, State Governments/Union Territories prepare their own plans and send them to the Planning Commission, which dovetails these schemes, programmes and projects into an integrated plan called the "Draft Plan". The draft plan is then released for public discussion.

The Third stage consists of prolonged discussions between the members of the Planning Commission and the representatives of different Central Ministries, State Governments and Union Territories, for arriving at an agreement on the nature and the size of the plans.

These tentative agreements are sent to the NDC after examination by the Union Cabinet. In the light of the recommendations of the NDC, the Planning Commission gives the final shape to the plan, which is placed before the Parliament for approval and subsequently becomes the official national plan.

Till date, the Planning Commission has drawn up seven Five Year Plans in addition to Annual Plans and Perspective Plans. Each Five Year Plan covers period of five years, beginning from the 1st April of the concerned year and ending on the 31st March of the fifth year.

Planning in India derives its objectives and social content from the Directive Principles of State Policy, which are enumerated in the Constitution. The basic objective of the Five Year Plans has been to secure a rapid and sustained economic growth and radical expansion of employment through most effective and balanced utilisation of country's resources. Its aim has been to ensure a fast reduction of disparities in income and wealth, thereby preventing concentration of economic power among a small number of people. It seeks to improve the living standards and working conditions of the toiling and denuded masses. It is the kingpin of a comprehensive strategy designed to bring about total self-reliance.

In the scheme of Indian Planning, the concept of mixed economy has been followed wherein the public and private sectors are considered complementary to each other. Social gains rather than personal enrichment form the crux of this philosophy.

The First Five Year Plan (1951-52 to 1955-56) was a "ground preparing" exercise which gave its primary attention to the achievement of economic stability and elimination of shortages of food and basic resources. Accordingly it accorded top priority to agriculture of which irrigation and power were deemed essential ingredients. About 44.6 per cent of the total outlay was earmarked for the agricultural sector. The annual growth targetted in this plan was 2.1 per cent of the national income.

The plan also aimed at increasing the rate of investment from five per cent to about seven per cent of the national income.

The Second Five Year Plan (1956-57 to 1960-61) aimed, among other things, at 25 per cent increase in the national income, rapid industrialisation with particular emphasis on development of basic and heavy industries, large expansion of employment opportunities and reduction of inequalities in income and wealth and more even distribution of economic power. The plan laid special premium on fastinating industrialisation with the aim of strengthening the capital base and productive capacity.

The Plan also aimed at increasing the rate of investment from about seven per cent of the national income to eleven per cent by 1960-61.

The Third Plan (1961-62 to 1965-66) aimed at securing a marked advance towards self-sustaining growth. Its immediate objectives were to (a) secure an increase in national income of over 5 per cent per annum and a simultaneous evolution of a pattern of investment capable of sustaining this rate of growth during subsequent plan period; (b) achieve self-sufficiency in food grains (the target of food grains production stood at 100 million tonnes) and increased agricultural production to meet the requirement of industry and exports; (c) expand basic industries like steel, chemicals, fuel and power and establish machine building capacity; (d) utilise fully manpower resources and ensure a substantial expansion of employment opportunities and (e) establish greater equality of opportunity and bring about reduction in disparities of income and wealth and more equitable dispersal of economic power. The plan sought to increase the national income by about 30 per cent from Rs.14,500 crore in 1960-61 to about Rs. 19,000 crore by 1965-66 (at 1960-61 prices) and per capita income by about 17 per cent from Rs. 300 to Rs. 385 during the same period.

The finalisation of the Fourth Five Year Plan was delayed on account of the situation created by the Indo-Pakistan War in 1965, two successive years of severe drought, devaluation of currency, general rise in prices and erosion of resources available for plan purposes. Therefore, three Annual Plans were formulated between 1966 and 1969.

The Fourth Five Year Plan (1969-70 to 1973-74) aimed at accelerating the tempo of development in conditions of stability and reducing the fluctuations in agricultural production as well as the impact uncertainties in foreign aid.

It sought to raise the standard of living and promote equality and social justice. The plan laid particular emphyasis on improving the conditions of the less-privilege and weaker sections of the society through gainful employment an education and on diluting the concentration through wider diffusion of wealth, income and economic power. The average annual rate of growth envisaged was 5.7 per cent.

The Fifth Plan (1974-75 to 1977-78) aimed at achieving self-reliance and adoption of measures to boom consumption standards of the people living below the poverty line. The plan also gave high priority to bringing inflation under control and achieving stability of the economic front. The Plan targetted an annual growth rate of 5.5 per cent in national income and better capacity utilisation of industries, developing renewable sources of energy, and integration of science and technology into the main stream of development. The Seventh Plan lays down an average annual growth rate target of 5 per cent. It also aims at a 8.7 per cent annual growth rate for industries.

The Sixth Plan (1980-81 to 1984-85) assigned the highest priority to the removal of poverty. The strategy was essentially to strengthen the infrastructure for both agriculture and industry so as to create conditions for a sustained and accelerated growth in investment output and exports. It aimed a meeting the minimum basic needs of the people through special programmes and creating increased opportunities for employment, especially in the rural areas and the unorganised sector. Stress was laid on greater management efficiency and intensive monitoring in all sectors and involvement of people in formulation and speedy implementation of schemes at the local level.

Fig. V.1A & B: Planning in India
Expenditure - Sector-wise

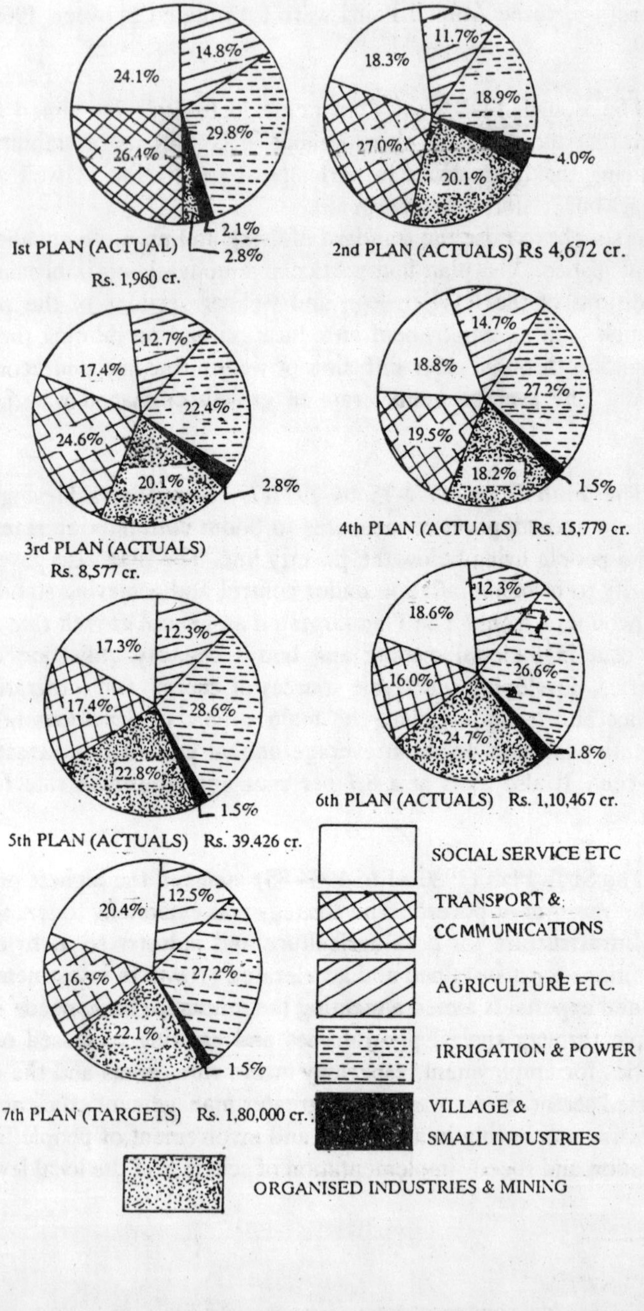

The Seventh Plan (1985-86 to 1989-90) gives highest priority to food, employment and productivity. Faster movement towards the objective of self-reliance with social justice is the core idea of the plan. The salient features of the plan are – decentralised planning, maximum employment generation, self sufficiency in food at higher levels of consumption, export-import balance, modernisation and upgradation of technology.

(Source: Yojana, October 1-15, 1988)

NEWS ABOUT PLANNING FROM PARLIAMENT[1]

The Minister of Planning and Programme Implementation, Shri Madhavsinh Solanki gave following information about plans and planning to Parliament during the monsoon session:

Draft Eight Plan

Under instructions from the Prime Minister as Chairman of the Planning Commission, the Commission is working on the implications of alternative higher growth scenarios for the 8th Five Year Plan. The related strategies will be set out in the Approach paper for the consideration of the National Development Council.

Industrial Planning

Apart from other areas of socio-economic activities, a greater thrust to industrial planning at State and District level is also envisaged in the Eighth Five Year Plan. This is in the process of discussion as an ongoing exercise in the Plan formulation. In addition to the National and State level Planning, the Government is examining the possibility of enlarging the scope of district level planning.

Rural Development Planning

The strategy laid down in the Seventh Five Year Plan (1985-86 to 1989-90) of accelerated agricultural growth, increased productivity of

----

1. *(Source: Yajana,*, October 1-15, 188)

rice in eastern India, developing the potential of dry land agriculture, adoption of special measures to increase productivity and incomes of small and marginal farmers, expansion of irrigation facilities, implementation of Minimum Needs Programme, and special anti-poverty and employment programmes specifically designed to raise incomes and productivity of the people below poverty line will be continued during the rest of the Seventh Plan period.

G.V.K. Rao Committee Report

Planning Commission has considered the report of the Committee headed by Shri G.V.K. Rao to review the existing administrative arrangements for rural development and poverty alleviation programmes. In due course of time, the matter will be placed before the National Development Council for consideration before final decisions are taken.

The main thrust of the report is on separation of development functions from regulatory functions at different levels, preparation of district plans, greater participation of voluntary organisations/ beneficiaries of planning and implementation of Rural Development Programmes and revamping of block level administration so as to achieve total delivery mechanism for rural development.

State Planning Boards

State Planning Boards have been constituted in all the States, except the States of Sikkim and Karnataka. In Karnataka however, there is a State level Economic and Planning Council.

The State Governments have been advised to strengthen their planning apparatus and they were requested to constitute an apex body at the State level with the Chief Minister as the Chairman and the Finance Minister, the Planning Minister, and the technical experts representing various departments and disciplines, as Members. Similarly, to facilitate planning at the district level, among other measures, States have been urged to set up District Planning Boards/Councils, with appropriate composition.

Disparity in Rural and Urban Income

The major thrust of planned growth in the country has been to reduce disparities in income. Almost all the points of the Twenty-Point Programme including Integrated Rural Development Programme (IRDP), National Rural Employment Programme (NREP) and Rural Landless Employment Guarantee Programme (RLEGP) are oriented towards the target groups in rural areas. These programmes target groups in rural areas. These programmes have been continued in the Seventh Five Year Plan with an accelerated pace with emphasis on agricultural growth, developing the potential of dry agriculture and adoption of special measures to increase the productivity of small and marginal farmers.

Minimum Needs Programme

The Seventh Plan outlay for Minimum Needs Programme is Rs. 11800.94 crore. The expenditure is likely to be within the outlay except in the Education Sector where new Programmes have been taken up for implementing the National Policy on Education.

Projects for Eighth Plan

First priority will be given to the expeditious completion of the on going schemes/projects as at the commencement of the 8th Plan. So far as new schemes/projects are concerned a decision will be taken in the light of intersectoral priorities set out in the Approach Paper of the Plan to be approved by the National Development Council.

Delay in Central Projects

According to the information available in the Ministry of Programme Implementation, some of the major projects, each costing over Rs. 100 crore in the power, fertilisers, coal and steel have suffered delays due to various factors including delays in land acquisition and in environmental clearances/equipment supply. The total investment anticipated in these projects is of the order of Rs. 25,000 crore.

Selected Targets (T) and Achievements (A): Successive Plans

Item	Unit	First Plan		Second Plan		Third Plan	
		T	A	T	A	T	A
Agriculture							
Foodgrains	Mn. tonnes	62.5	66.9	81.8	82.0	101.6	72.3
Oilseeds	-do-	5.6	5.7	7.7	7.0	10.0	6.4
Sugarcane (Gur)	-do-	6.4	6.1	7.9	11.1	10.2	12.8
Cotton	Mn. bales	4.1	4.0	6.4	5.3	6.9	4.6
Irrigation and power							
Net irrigated area	Mn. hectares	—	22.8	27.5	24.6	36.4	26.3
Electricity installed capacity	Mn. kw	3.6	3.4	7.1	5.6	12.7	10.2
Mining and manufacturing							
Iron ore	Mn. tonnes	4.1	4.3	12.7	11.0	32.5	18.1
Coal (including lignite)	-do-	39.6	39.9	61.0	55.5	98.6	70.3
Finished steel	-do-	1.7	1.3	4.4	2.4	6.8	4.5
Machine tools	Rs. crores	—	0.8	3.0	7.0	30.0	29.4
Cement	Mn. tonnes	4.9	4.7	13.2	8.0	13.0	10.8
Petroleum products	-do-	4.1	3.7	4.4	5.8	9.9	9.4
Fertiliser production	'000 tonnes	121	92	418	150	1,200	344
Cloth (mill-made)	Crore metres	430	466	489	465	530	440
Sugar	Mn. tonnes	1.5	1.7	2.3	2.7	3.5	3.5

(Contd.)

(Contd. Table **Selected Targets (T) and Achievements (A): Successive Plans**

Item	Unit	First Plan		Second Plan		Third Plan	
		T	A	T	A	T	A
Transport and communications							
Surfaced roads	'000 kms.	–	209	229	263	276	343
Railway originating freight traffic	Mn. tonnes	–	115.9	164.6	156.2	248.9	203.0
Shipping (coastal & overseas)	Lakh GRT	6.0	4.8	9.0	9.0	10.4	15.4
Post offices	'000	55	55	75	77	100	97
Telephones	Lakhs	2.7	2.8	4.6	4.6	7.6	8.6
Social services							
Primary schools	'000	–	278	331	330	406	391
Middle schools	'000	–	23	25	50	58	76
Hospital-beds	'000	–	125	155	186	240	240
Doctors	'000	–	65	70	70	81	86
Nurses	'000	–	18	31	27	45	45

(*Source :* *CSO, Statistical Abstract 1984; Statistical Pocket Book 1984; The Seventh Five Year Plan, 1985-90.*)

Annual Plans	Fourth Plan		Fifth Plan (Terminal year 1977-78)		Sixth Plan		Seventh Plan
A	T	A	T	A	T	A[a]	T
94.0	129.0	104.7	118.0	126.4	153.6	150.0	178-183
6.8	10.0	8.9	10.8	9.6	13.0	13.0	18.0
12.8	15.0	14.4	155.0	182.0	215	180.0	217.0
5.1	8.0	6.3	7.0	7.1	8.5	7.5	9.5
27.7*	43.0	42.2	53.3	50.7	64.7	67.9	80.8
14.3	23.6	18.6	27.0	26.0	45.1	42.5	64.7
19.9*	51.4	35.7	56.0	40.9	45.0	42.2	58.1
72.8*	93.5	81.8	128.5	101.0	173.0	155.2	241.2
4.4*	8.1	4.4	7.4	7.0	9.0	8.8	12.6
29.8*	65.0	67.3	125.0	102.7	302.0	303.0	500.0
11.6*	18.0	14.7	19.7	19.3	32.5	30.1	49.0
13.7*	26.0	19.5	24.1	23.1	34.2	33.3	45.5
588*	3,400	1,383	3,000	2,638	4,875	5,181	8,750
425*	510	408	425	418	400	342	450
2.7	4.7	3.7	5.2	6.4	7.6	6.2	10.2
393	450	499	—	596	—	833	—
204.0	240.5	184.9	—	237.3	309.0	264.4	340
7.1*	35.0	30.9	—	53.8	75.0	63.3	75.0
102	119	117	124	125	145	145	—
10.7	17.8	16.4	22.9	22.5	43.4	34.6	—
399	—	430	—	463	—	550	—
84	—	97	—	110	—	410	—
256	282	282	322	314	382	N.A	—
103	138	138	176	170	246	272	—
61	88	88	123	108	174	163	—

a - Anticipated actual production of 1984-85.

* - Average for three years (1966-69).

— - Targets not fixed.

N.A. - Not available.

Plan Outlays : Minimum Needs Programme

(Rs. crores)

Programme	Sixth Plan outlay 1980-85	Expenditure 1980-85	Seventh Plan outlay 1985-90	Expenditure 1985-86	1986-87**
Elementary education	851.00 +54.00	827.96 +62.11	1,730.45 +100.00	268.57	466.04
Adult education	68.00 +60.00	70.72 +95.70	230.00 +130.00	62.15	100.73
Rural health	408.00 +169.00	383.29 +183.17	1,063.35 +30.00	129.06	174.23
Rural water supply	1,407.00 +600.00	1,497.90 +908.66	2,235.25 +1,201.22	700.93	762.25
Rural electrification	301.00	249.25	497.08	58.42	95.92
Rural roads	1,165.00	1,261.96	1,729.40	252.79	290.17
Rural housing	354.00	426.54	576.90	102.85	142.24
Improvement of urban slums	151.80	150.93 +32.00	269.55	44.87	44.73
Nutrition	219.00	397.13	1,732.86	175.28	282.84
Total: State sector	4,924.00	5,265.33	10,078.72		
Total: Central sector	+833.00	+1,769.89	+1,464.22		
Grand total	5,807.00	7,035.22	11,542.94		

(*Source:* *Seventh Five Year Plan, 1985-90.*)

* = Including anticipated expenditure for 1984-85.
\+ = Represents Central outlay/expenditure.
** = Anticipated.

Note: Blank spaces indicate non-availability of data.

Delay in Project Completion

As on 31st March, 1988, 319 central projects, each costing over Rs. 20 crores in 14 sectors are under the Quarterly Monitoring System.The total cost of all these projects taken together as anticipated at the end of March, 1988, showed an increase of 48 per cent in relation to the total originally approved cost.

Thirty Five projects put back their commissioning dates in 1987-88. One hundred and thirty one projects have reported additional delays during 1987-88. Some of these projects have reported delays more than once during the year.

CHAPTER 6

STATE OF ECONOMY

Followng three important documents indicate the state of Indian economy:

1. Reserve Bank Report 1988-89.
2. Report of the Central Statistical Organisation 1987-88.
3. World Bank Report 1988.

Reserve Bank Report 1988-89

Industrial Output

According to the report of the Reserve Bank for the year 1988-89, during the first six months (April-September, 1988), industrial output grew by 9.4 per cent which was somewhat lower than that of 10.9 per cent during the correspondence period of 1987-88. The sectoral trend in industrial production during this period suggests that with the exception of 'mining and quarrying' which showed a marginal acceleration in growth rate from 5.3 per cent to 5.7 per cent, the growth rate in the other two sectors, viz. 'manufacturing' and 'electricity' showed sharp deceleration to 10.6 per cent and 6.0 per cent compared with 12.2 per cent and 9.3 per cent, respectively, during the corresponding period of 1987-88.

Agricultural Production

Taking both foodgrains and non-foodgrains production, the total agricultural production was expected to show a rise of about 20 per cent during 1988-89.

Foreign Debt in 1988

India borrowed foreign exchange worth Rs. 4,619 crore and of that, debt servicing consumed Rs. 2,579 crore (55.83%). The interest component alone was Rs. 10,33 crore. Debt servicing amount went up by 27 per cent (Rs. 550 crore) in 1988 alone.

Decline of the Rupee

There was a great decline of the rupee in the world market. During 1988, the Rupee depreciated against other major currencies, DM 14.9%, yen 14.8%, pound sterling 13.7%, U.S. Dollar 1.5%.

Inflation

The inflationary pressures were more pronounced at the retail level than at the wholesale level during 1988. The price increase on a point to point basis under the consumer Price Index for industrial worker (Base 1960-100) up to November 1988 at 10 per cent was higher as compared with a rise of 4.2 per cent in the wholesale Price Index for the same period.

Budget Deficit

The revenue expenditure at the Centre rose at a faster pace than revenue receipts. The deficit on revenue account was estimated to enlarge to Rs. 9,842 crores for 1988-89, as compared with Rs. 8,497 crores in 1987-88. After taking into account, the overall deficit was budgetted at Rs.7,484 crores in 1988-89 as compared with Rs. 6,080 crores in the previous year.

Trade Deficit

Debt servicing and heavy import continued to mount and cost the country heavily in terms of foreign exchange. During the period April-December 1988, foreign exchange reserves declined by Rs 1,052 crore as against Rs.528 crore in the corresponding period of 1987. The situation reached such a delicate point that the level of foreign exchange reserves at the end of Dec. 1988, was equivalent to less than three months of imports.

The trade deficit, during April-October 1988, had widened to Rs 4,936 crore from Rs. 3,484 crore in the corresponding period of 1987, mainly due to a rise in imports. Exports increased to Rs.15,719 crore in 1987-88 against the figure of Rs.12,550 crore for 1986-87 while imports totalled Rs. 22,343 crore in 1987-88, showing an increase of Rs. 2,259 crore in one year. The foreign exchange assets of Reserve Bank of India alone fell by Rs.1,468 crore during the first quarter (April-June) of 1988-89 – the fall-figure for the corresponding quarter of 1987-88 was only Rs.369 crore

Savings and Investment

The estimates present a somewhat dismaying picture of the trend in savings and investment in the economy. For the third successive year, there was a decline in both. The gross savings rate (expressed as a percentage of gross domestic product) declined from 22 per cent in 1985-86 to 21.6 per cent in 1986-87 and further down to 20.2 per cent in 1987-88. The net savings rate similarly shows a decline between 1986-87 and 1987-88 from 12.7 per cent to 11.1 per cent. The sectorwise contributions to domestic savings shows that while both the private corporate and the household sector showed an increase in their savings, the net dissaving by the public sector, showed a whopping increase of 71.37 per cent while the dissaving in administration increased from (-) Rs.2199 crore to (-) Rs.5725 crore implying an increase of 160 per cent. The deficit in the government's accounts had widened considerably during the year. The investment rate shows a decline from 24.4 per cent of gross domestic product in 1985-86 to 23.4 per cent in 1986-87 and further down to 22.1 per cent in 1987-88. Net capital formation declined by 1.2 per cent in the same period, while the decline when compared to the rate of net investment in 1985-86 shows a decline of 2.6 per cent.

Bank Deposits

The Scheduled Commercial Banks operations during 1988-89 (upto December 30, 1988) were characterised by a sharp rise in aggregate deposits. Accretion to aggregate deposits of scheduled commercial banks during the financial year 1988-89 (upto December 30) was Rs. 21,394 crores (18.1%) as against a rise of Rs. 17,402 crores (16.9%) during the comparable period of 1987-88.

Fig. VI.1

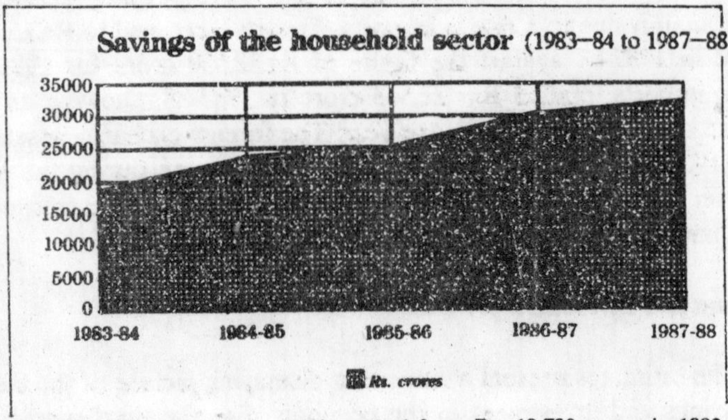

The savings of the houshold sector increased from Rs. 18,790 crores in 1983-84 to Rs. 32,433 crores in 1987-88. This was about 11 per cent of net domestic product. Bank deposits accounted for the bulk (36.1 per cent) of household savings, followed by providend and pension funds (18.15 per cent) in 1987-88. Interest in units has been growing over the years, and while in 1983-84 it accounted for 1.2 per cent of total savings, in 1987-88 it had grown to 4.7 per cent.
(*Source: Business India*, January 23 – February 5, 1989)

The spurt in investment activity was reflected in a sharp increase of 77.6 per cent in financial assistance sanctioned by the All India term lending institution during April–September 1988.

The average index equity prices recorded a rise of 6.7 per cent during April-November 1988 in contrast to a decline of 9.8 per cent during the correspondence period of the preceding year.

Report of the Reserve Bank of India on Currency and Finance[1]

The foodgrain production in the current year (1988-89) is expected to total 31 million tonnes higher than the previous year, the industrial sector will show an upturn, with improved availability of agricultural raw materials.

The relatively low level of public sector stock of foodgrains, the larger budget deficit and the current account deficit are, "area of concern".

---

1. *Source*: The Hindustan Times, February 1, 1989)

Fig. VI.2

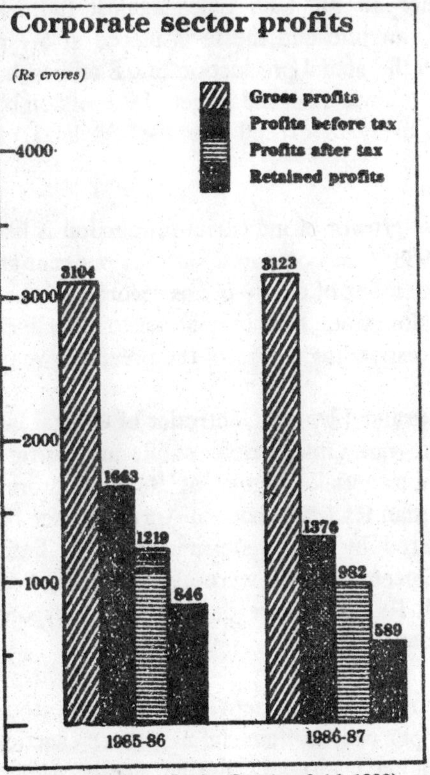

Source: (Business India: October 3-16, 1988)

The reports states that the Indian Economy has acquired resilience over the years, as was proved by the fact that while in the past drought year, real income tended to decline, the country recorded positive growth in 1987-88 as the decline in agricultural output was less sharp than feared and industrial production showed a reasonable growth despite the drought of exceptional magnitude and severity.

It says commercial crops prospects are also encouraging. The groundnut growing areas of Gujarat are reported to have received good rains, promising a bumper kharif oilseeds harvest of eight million tonnes as against 6.3 million tonnes last year. Oilseeds production could very well be in the range of 15-16 million tonnes as against

12.4 million tonnes. Raw cotton production is expected to be substantially higher at 102 lakh bales against (90 lakh bales), the production of raw jute and mesta is placed at 6-7 million bails as compared with the actual production of 6.8 million bales in 1987-88, but substantially lower than the target of 9.2 million bales. Sugarcane production is likely to exceed the 1987-88 level of 196.7 million tonnes.

The ratio of growth of industrial production is likely to exceed 9 per cent for 1988-89 as compared with 7.7 per cent attained in 1987-88. The average index of equity prices recorded a rise of 6.7 per cent during April–November 1988 in contrast to a decline of 9.8 per cent during the corresponding period of the preceding year.

Approvals granted by the Controller of Capital Issues for raising fresh capital to non-Government public and private limited companies were substantially higher at Rs.2,110 crore during April-October 1988 than Rs.1,503 crore in April-October 1987. Fresh capital issues offered by non-Government public limited companies during April-December 1988 were also higher at Rs. 1,759 crore as compared with Rs.1,398 crore during the corresponding period of the previous year.

The spurt in investment activity is also reflected in a sharp increase of 77.6 per cent in financial assistance sanctioned by the all-India term-lending institutions during April-September 1988. The overall growth of liquidity during the current financial year up to December 30, was Rs.24,179 crore (14.9%) as compared with Rs.21,207 crore (15.1%) during the comparable period of 1987-88. With buoyant agricultural output following the good monsoon, the growth of real national income in 1988-89 is expected to be of the order of 9 per cent.

Reserve Bank of India points out that in the fiscal sphere, with the revenue expenditure of the Centre rising at a faster pace than revenue receipts, the deficit on revenue account is estimated to enlarge to Rs.9,842 crore for 1988-89 (Rs.8,497 crore). After taking into account the surplus on capital account, the overall deficit is budgeted at Rs.7,484 crore in 1988-89 as compared with Rs.6,080 crore in the previous year. The deterioration in the Central finances is mainly due to a sharp rise in non-plan expenditure, particularly under interest payments, defence and subsidies.

Preliminary data on the collection of tax revenues from major taxes available for the eight months (April-November) of the current financial year show an increase of Rs. 2,635 crore, constituting 58.9 per cent of the anticipated increase for 1988-89. Collections from direct taxes, i.e. income and corporation taxes, were higher by 6.7 per cent over the corresponding period of last year. The expenditure of the Central Government is expected to be higher than that estimated in the budget.

Of this, the expenditure on non-plan account would be Rs.678 crore and the remaining Rs. 640 crore would be on plan account.

In the current financial year so far, there has been a deceleration in the pace of reserve money growth (12.2 per cent against 15.9 per cent). The overhang of large reserve money creation of the previous three years provides a potential for expansion in over all liquidity.

The operations of scheduled commercial banks during the current financial year (up to Dec.30) have been characterised by a sharp rise in aggregate deposits. Accretion to aggregate deposits was Rs. 21,394 crore (18.1%) as against a rise of Rs. 17,402 crore (16.9%) during the comparable period of the previous year. Demand deposits showed a sharp increase of Rs.3,627 crore (Rs. 2,505 crore). Time deposits increase by Rs. 17,767 crore (Rs. 14,897 crore). There has been a large increase in net non-food credit of Rs. 10,420 crore (15.2%). The comparable figure for 1987-88 was Rs.8,917 crore (15.3%).

Report of Central Staistical Organisation[2]
3.6 per cent Rise in GDP in 1987-88

Gross Domestic Product (GDP) and national income rose by 3.6 per cent and 3.4 per cent during 1987-88 financial year, according to Central Statistical Organisation, Planning Ministry.

---

2. (*Source:* Report of central statistical organisation, *The Hindustan Times*, January 29, 1989)

GDP at a factor cost at constant (1980-81) prices in 1987-88 is estimated at 1,70,363 crore as against Rs. 1,64,441 crore in 1986-67, showing an increase of 3.6 per cent during the year.

At current prices, the GDP in 1987-88 is estimated at Rs.2,93,306 crore as against Rs. 2,60,680 crore in the previous year, an increase of 12.5 per cent, according to the quick estimates of nationaal income and related aggregates for fiscal 1987-88.

At constant prices the total National 'Income (i.e net national product at factor cost) in 1987-88 is estimated at Rs.1,50,573 crore as against Rs.1,45,675 crore in 1986-87 showing a rise of 3.4 per cent during the year.

The estimates say that the slightly lower growth rate of national income compared with that of GDP is mainly because of higher level of consumption of fixed capital.

At current prices, the national income in 1987-88 is estimated at Rs.2,57,813 crore as compared to Rs.2,29,010 crore in 1986-87, a rise of 12.6 per cent during the year.

The following figures shows the State of G.D.P. over the Year

	1980-81	1985-86	1986-87	1987-88
1. Gross Domestic Product at factor cost (Rs. crore)				
(i) at current prices	1,22,226	2,33,305	2,60,680	2,93,306
(ii) at 1980-81 prices	1,22,226	1,56,083	1,64,441	1,70,363
2. Net National Product at factor cost viz., National Income (Rs. crore)				
(i) At current prices	1,10,484	2,05,436	2,29,010	2,57,813
(ii) at 1980-81 prices	1,10,484	1,38,611	1,45,675	1,50,573
3. Per capita National Income (Rs)				
(i) at current prices	1,627.2	2,721.0	2,974.5	3,223
(ii) at 1980-81 prices	1,627.2	1,835.9	1,869.3	1,882

Fig. VI.3. Gross Domestic Product 1980-81 to 1987-88
(At 1980-81 Prices in Rs. crores)

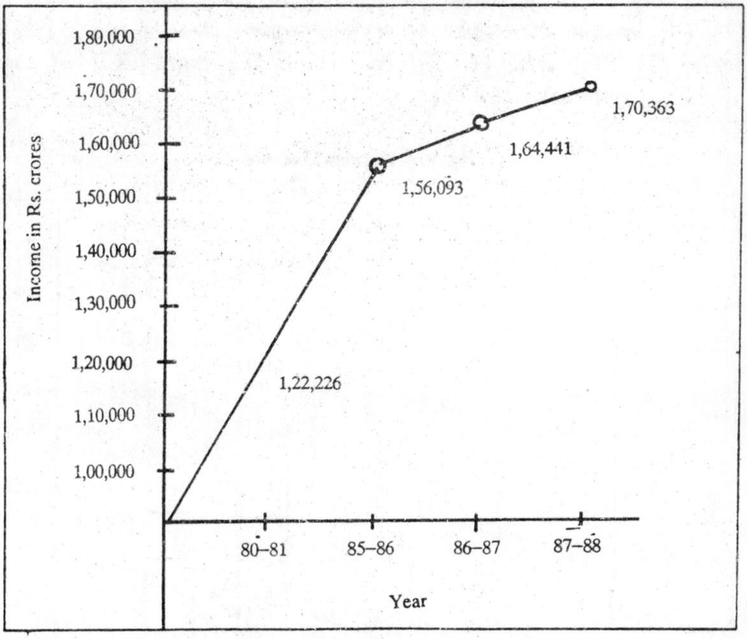

The Central Statistical Organization (CSO) said in order to derive the gross domestic product at market prices so that it equals the expenditure on gross domestic product, the GDP at factor cost is adjusted by adding indirect taxes net of subsidies. As the various components of gross domestic expenditure, for example, consumption expenditure and capital formation, are normally measured at market prices, the following estimates had been done in terms of market prices only.

Private final consumption expenditure at current prices works out to Rs. 2,21,057 crore in 1987-88 forming 66.9 per cent of the gross domestic product at market prices.

The per capita expenditure during the year works out to Rs. 2,816 at current prices as against Rs. 2,578 during the previous year and Rs. 1,709 at constant (1980-81) prices as against Rs.1,677 during the previous year.

There was a fall of 3.5 per cent in the production of foodgrains from 143.4 million tonnes in 1986-87 to 138.4 million tonnes in 1987-88, mainly attributable to decline in production of rice (6.8 %), gram (20.1 %), arhar (1.6 %), bajra (27.3 %), maize (26.9 %), ragi (14.2 %) and barley (4.6 %).

Fig. VI.4. National Income

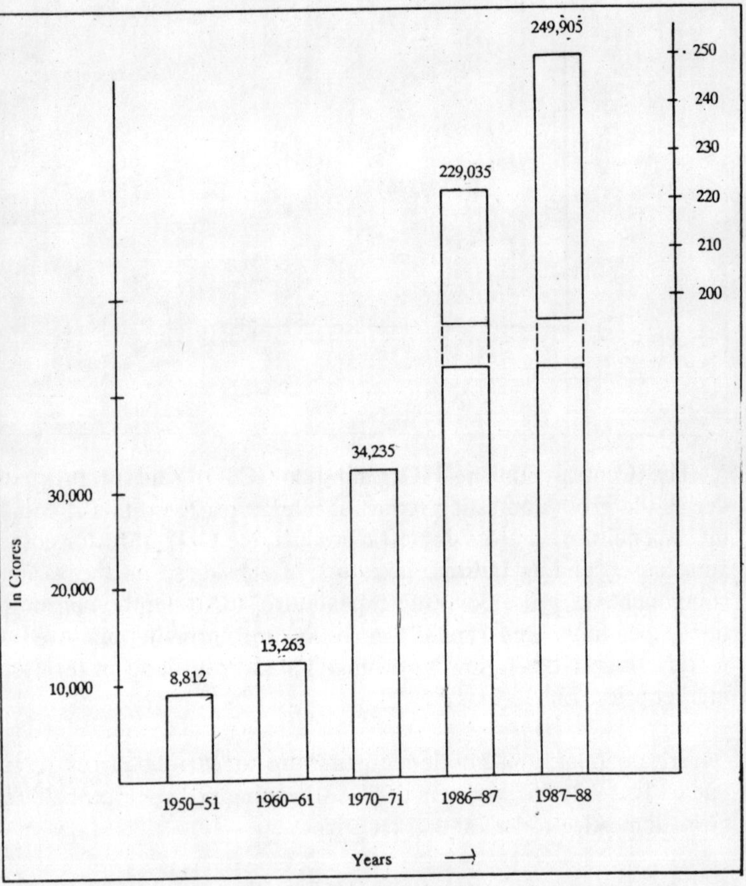

The estimates say that in the case of other crops, there was an increae in the production of oilseeds (9.8 %), sugarcane (5.7 %) and potato (11 %), while there was a decline in production of kapas (6.9 %), tobacco (22.3 %), and jute (21.8 %).

In Animal Husbandry there was an increase of 1.2 per cent in the value of output as against four per cent during 1986-87. This has resulted in an overall fall of 1.1 per cent in net value added in agriculture as against a fall of 2.3 per cent observed during 1986-87.

The Central Statistical Organization said forestry also registered a decline of 2.5 per cent. All other industries registered a positive growth rate. These industries either maintained the growth rate achieved in 1985-87 (for example, construction, real estate, ownership, ownership of dwellings and business services, transport by other means and other services) or achieved somewhat lower rate as compared to 1986-87.

Indian Economy

The World Bank in its Annual Report 1988, lauded India in 'these words, ". . . . . despite the severe shortage of rainfall and decline in crop production, food stocks and food distribution were adequate to avert widespread hunger and starvation. Real GDP growth is now estimated at about 1.8 per cent for fiscal year 1988, down from 4 per cent last year, but considerably better than the 4.9 per cent decline registered during the drought of 1979.[3] Because of the effect of drought on agricultural prices, inflation neared 10 per cent for the first time since the early 1980s.

India's success in averting the worst effects of the drought was due to timely action by the government and the existence of well-established institutional mechanisms for coping with such emergencies. The government's programme included emergency-relief measures, as well as steps to salvage what production could be saved and to ensure the best possible production at the next planting. Both central and state governments increased their ongoing public-works and relief programmes in an effort to maintain the purchasing power of the poorer groups. The central government also moved to maintain availability of basic foods and contain price increases by drawing down its food-grain stocks, and by importing edible oils, pulses, and fodder.

---

3. India's fiscal year runs from April 1 to March 31.

India was supported by the Bank in this effort through a drought-assistance project, and by special credits and assistance provided by bilateral donors. The Bank project provided $ 350 million to finance, on a fast-disbursing basis, imports of agroindustrial inputs, petroleum and petroleum products, nonferrous metals, as well as industrial equipment and spare parts. By far the largest portion of the total cost of this effort, however, was financed by the government. In addition to the assistance for India's drought recovery, Bank lending in fiscal 1988 continued its significant role in various sectors, including energy, transport, health and population, finance, and agriculture.

Overall, the government's capacity to manage successfully and finance a massive emergency-relief programme is strong testimony to the development progress that India has made over the past twenty five years. Yet, the challenges that lie ahead are still enormous by any measure. Population growth is high, and despite advances in raising standards of living among the poor, those living in absolute poverty still number roughly 270 million. Demographic pressures will strain the cpacity of the government both to expand social services and preserve fiscal and external balances.

Basic Indicators

Poverty Alleviation

The implementation of poverty alleviation programmes is the corner stone of country's planned development strategy. Some ten crore people have been brought above the poverty line in the last few years. The Lok Sabha was informed on August 3, 1988 that persons living below the poverty line in the country upto March 1985 were 271 million constituting 37.4 per cent of the total population. The Seven Plan aims at bringing the poverty ratio to 25.8 per cent.

National Income

National income, a composite measure of all economic activities taking place in an economy is a comprehensive index of the state of an economy and a measure of its growth over time. Despite its limitation it is used to compare the economic progress of a country with other countries of the world. National income of India during the years has been as under:

Year	National Income (Rs. crores)
1950-51	8,812
1960-61	13,263
1970-71	34,235
1986-87	2,29,035
1987-88	2,49,905

(*Source*: Tata Statistical Outline 1988-1989)

Fig. VI.5. Per Capita National Income 1980-81 to 1987-88 (At 1980-81 Prices in Rs.)

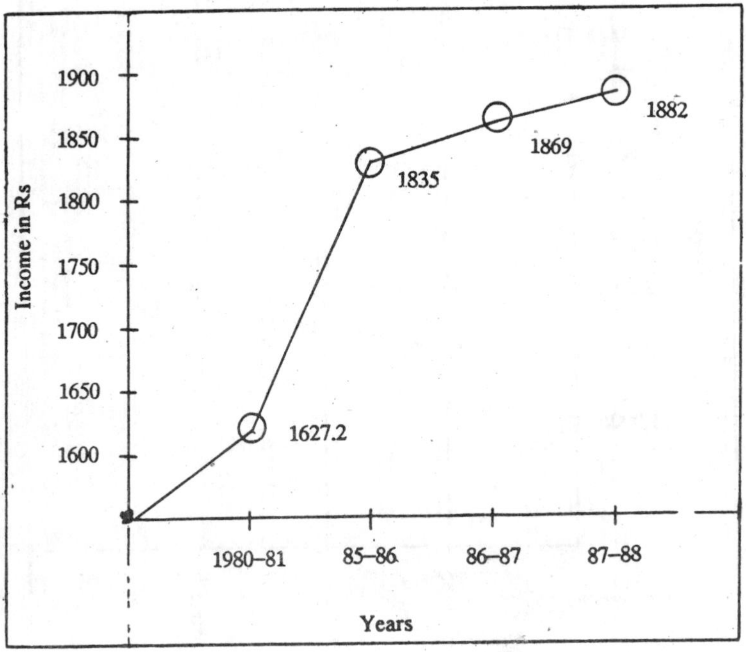

Fig. VI.6. Per Capita Income (At Current Prices) Delhi and Bihar (Highest and Lowest)

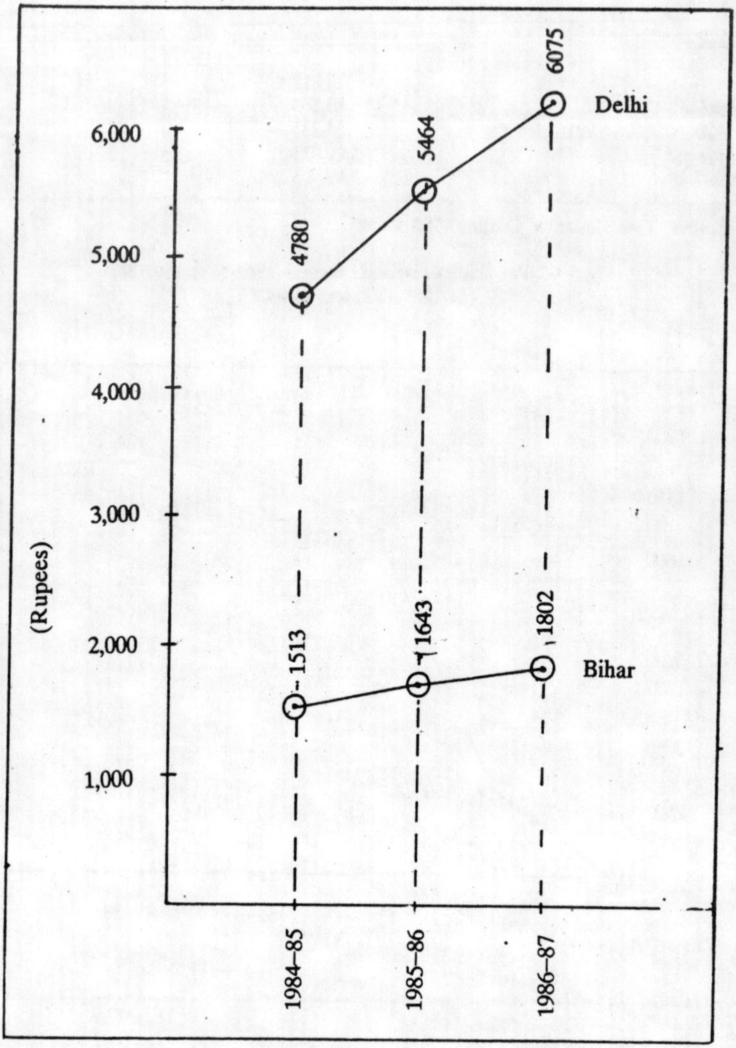

State/Union Territorywise Per Capita Income (At Current Prices)

(Rupees)

Sl.No.	State/U.T.	1984-85	1985-86	1986-87
1.	Delhi	4780	5464	6075
2.	Punjab	4075	4479	4719
3.	Goa*	4492	4782	NA
4.	Pondicherry	3736	3810	3994
5.	Haryana	3230	3748	3925
6.	Maharashtra	3137	3549	3793
7.	Arunachal Pradesh	2301	2834	NA
8.	Gujarat	2952	2775	3223
9.	West Bengal	2576	2767	2988
10.	Sikkim	2559	NA	NA
11.	Himachal Pradesh	2216	2636	2908
12.	Tamil Nadu	2173	2514	2732
13.	Manipur	2218	2383	2533
14.	Karnataka	2189	2264	2486
15.	Kerala	2104	2140	2371
16.	Jammu and Kashmir	2111	2270	2344
17.	Andhra Pradesh	2039	2205	2333
18.	Assam	2037	2068	2204
19.	Rajasthan	2050	2106	2150
20.	Tripura	1980	2065	NA
21.	Mizoram	1793	NA	NA
22.	Uttar Pradesh	1784	2003	2146
23.	Meghalaya	1872	2114	NA
24.	Madhya Pradesh	1699	1960	2020
25.	Orissa	1671	1954	1957
26.	Bihar	1513	1643	1802
27.	Nagaland	NA	NA	NA

* Figures in respect of Goa relate to erstwhile Wnion Territory of Goa, Daman & Diu.

NA Indicate Not available

<u>Inflation Rate</u> <u>Year ending March</u>

Year	Rate of Inflation
1985	7.6%
1986	3.8%
1987	5.3%
1988 (April-September)	10.6%

Purchasing Power of the Rupee
1970-71 to January 1988
(1960 = 100 Paise)

Year	Purchasing Power (Paise)
1970-71	54.35
1975-76	34.97
1980-81	23.81
1985-86	15.67
1986-87	14.57
January 1988	13.29

Whole Sale Price Index
1987-88 and 1988-1989
Base 1970-71 = 100

	1987-88 (December 19)	1988-89 (December 17)	%Increase over the Year
All Commodities	409.4	434.4	6.10%
Primary Articles	388.2	417.7	7.60%
Mfg. Articles	388.1	407.0	4.87%

Index Number of Wholesale Prices
Trends (All Commodities)

	Financial year average index		
	Base 1952-53 = 100	Base 1961-62 = 100	Base 1970-71 = 100
1950-51	107.7	86.1	47.5
1955-56	92.5	73.9	40.8
1960-61	124.5	99.8	55.1
1965-66	165.0	131.6	72.7
1970-71	226.6	181.1	100.0
1971-72	235.7	188.4	105.6
1972-73	259.1	207.1	116.2
1973-74	318.0	254.2	139.7
1974-75	391.6	313.0	174.9
1975-76	378.8	302.8	173.0
1976-77	388.7	310.7	176.6
1977-78	421.0	336.5	185.8
1978-79	421.0	336.3	185.8
1979-80	493.0	394.1	217.6
1980-81	583.0	466.0	257.3
1981-82	637.3	509.4	281.3
1982-83	654.0	522.8	288.7
1983-84	715.9	572.3	316.0
1984-85	766.6	612.8	338.4
1985-86	810.6	648.0	357.8
1986-87	853.7	682.4	376.8

(*Source: Wholesale Prices in India. Monthly Bulletin, March 1987.*)

Fig. VI.7. Whole Sale Prices in India 1950-51 to 1986-87 Trends (All Commodities)

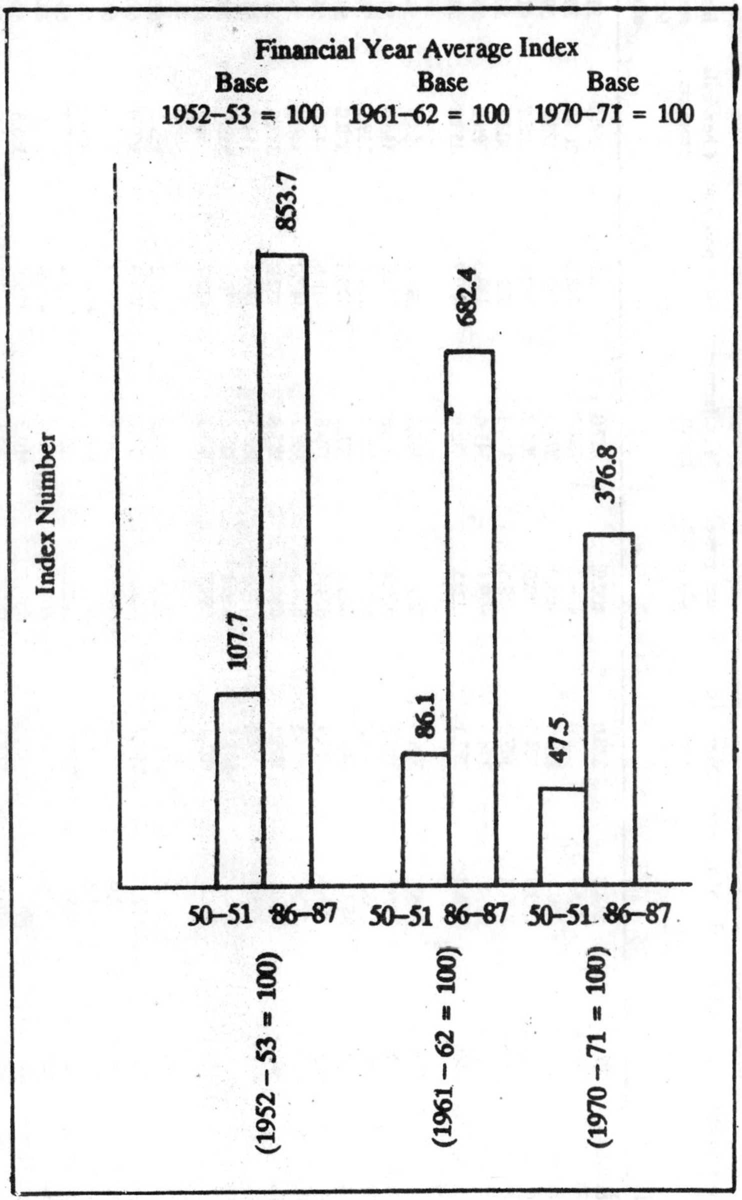

Wholesale Price Index

Week ended	All commodities	Food articles	Non-food articles	Fuel, power, light & lub.	Manufactured goods	Food products	Chemicals products	Iron & steel ferro alloys
1980-81	257.3	218.0	228.0	400.0	267.0	313.0	254.0	313.3
1981-82	281.3	235.0	233.0	438.0	264.0	248.0	264.0	354.0
1982-83	288.7	250.0	250.0	484.0	275.0	247.0	273.0	399.0
1983-84	316.1	283.0	304.0	509.0	301.0	298.1	285.1	419.1
1984-85	338.4	276.2	307.0	559.6	330.8	321.7	303.8	535.1
1985-86	357.8	319.1	274.9	609.1	341.6	338.3	320.2	541.0
Dec. 10, 1987	408.7	374.0	397.1	635.5	385.6	459.9	353.8	545.4
1987								
Jan.	378.3	338.1	328.3	621.5	363.5	385.4	334.5	542.5
March	378.2	341.4	319.8	626.2	362.3	365.0	336.4	544.9
May	389.7	356.7	344.5	626.2	370.8	390.8	339.1	544.9
June	391.3	357.2	349.6	626.2	372.5	398.3	339.9	544.9
July	401.5	364.8	384.0	634.4	379.8	419.8	342.0	544.9
August	410.9	373.4	409.3	634.5	388.1	447.0	346.8	544.9
Sep.	405.9	368.8	386.2	634.5	385.8	432.2	353.0	545.4
Oct.	410.0	373.3	397.2	634.5	388.5	437.7	354.1	545.4
Nov.	411.1	376.4	402.5	636.1	387.6	430.0	352.7	545.4
Dec., 1987	413.1	368.4	403.4	654.9	393.2	423.7	360.2	611.5
1988								
Jan.	415.4	371.9	407.4	622.8	393.5	416.2	359.0	628.2
Feb.	413.5	372.2	397.7	664.9	391.1	396.3	360.6	628.2
March	413.8	372.6	398.8	667.6	390.9	391.9	359.2	631.5
April	416.9	377.2	389.6	667.6	396.1	400.5	361.0	631.5
May 28	423.1	386.6	391.2	668.0	402.7	409.4	365.4	634.3
June 25	427.2	391.6	390.4	669.1	407.8	426.8	366.2	634.3
July	429.9	394.9	391.9	669.1	410.9	436.9	366.3	634.3
Oct. 8	439.1	410.9	376.5	671.3	422.1	459.9	373.9	644.7

Fig. VI.8. Commodity Prices : 1988
Whoesale Price Index Base 1969-70

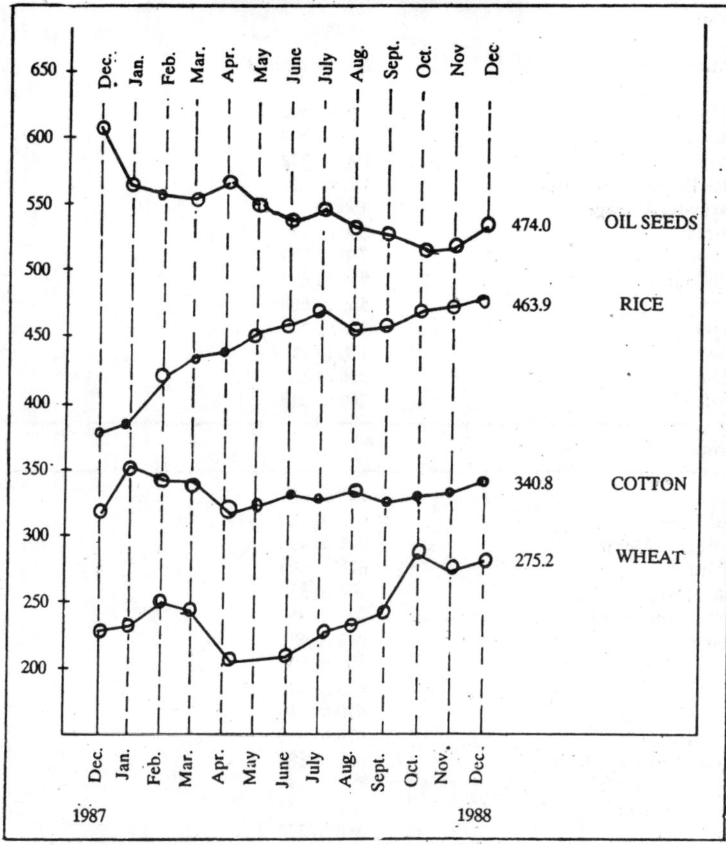

Fig. VI.9. Consumer Price Index for Industrial Workers
October 1987 to September 1988
(1960-61 = 100)

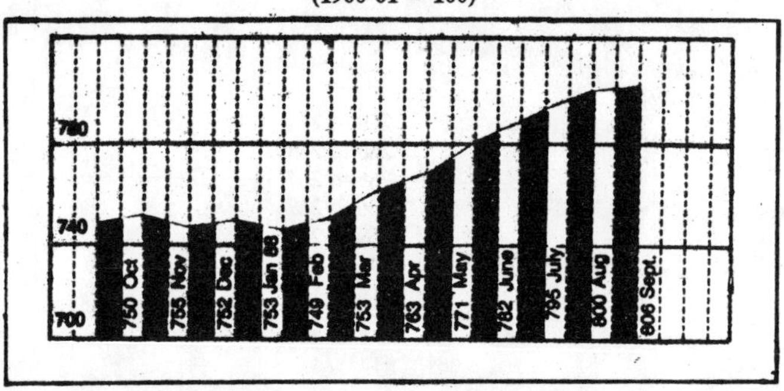

Grains Prices (Rs. per quintal) December 31, 1988

Delhi

Grains	*Rs. per quintal*
Wheat Desi	325 to 400
Kalyan	300 to 305
Dara	290 to 292
Rice Basmati (Superior)	1875
Basmati (Average)	1500
Permal	330 to 470
Gram	740 to 770
Kabli Gram	840 to 880
Peas	580 to 600
Bajra	150 to 210
Jowar	170 to 250
Maize	210 to 235
Barley	200 to 210
Pulses	
Urad	490 to 620
Dal Urad	650 to 825
Dal Urad Dhoia	725 to 900
Moong	625 to 690
Dal Moong	700 to 850
Dal Moong Dhoia	800 to 950
Masoor	640 to 680
Dal Masor	700 to 800
Moth	470 to 490
Arhar	470 to 520
Dal Arhar	670 to 800
Gram Dal	840 to 880
Gur and Sugar	
Gur	350 to 370
Sugar Desi	640 to 665
Khandsari	515 to 610

Moga

Grains and Pulses	
Wheat Farm	268 to 271
Sharbati	266 to 268
Dara	265 to 267
Mexican	266 to 269
Kalyan	269 to 272
Gram Black	745 to 765

Oil Prices at Delhi Rs. per quintal (December 31, 1988)

Oilseeds	
Mustardseed	550 to 600
Groundnut	550 to 700
Cottonseed	320 to 430
Sesame	725 to 860
Toria	400 to 500
Oils	
Vanaspati	341 to 357
Groundnut Mill Delivery	1680
Solvent Refined (per tin)	295 to 306
Refined (per tin)	340 to 390
Mustard Pakkighani (per tin)	267 to 270
Kachhighani (per tin)	285 to 295
Seasame Mill Delivery	1,680
Seasame (per tin)	320
Soyabean Mill Delivery	1,540
Refined (per tin)	316 to 340
Cottonseed Mill Delivery	1,550
Mahuwa	1,650 to 1,800
Coconut (per tin)	575
Linseed	1,600 to 1,610
Castor	1,450 to 1,460
Neem	1,140 to 1,150
Rice Bran Oil	1,030 to 1,040

Fig. VI.10. Per Capita Consumption

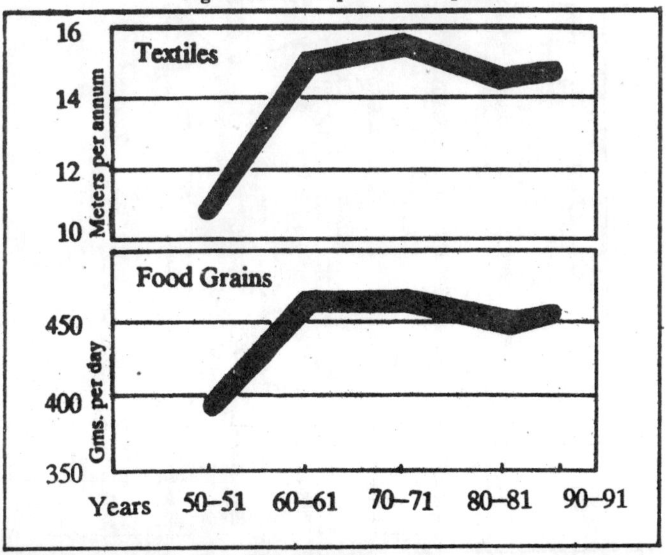

(*Source: Tata statistical outline* 1988–89)

Exports and Imports

On May 20, the Finance and Commerce Minister released the provisional export and import figures for 1987-88. Exports increased by 24 per cent and imports by 11.8 per cent. The exports stood at Rs.15,719 crore-exceeding the target set for the year by Rs.1,919 crore. The imports accounted for Rs.22,343.02 crore.

Fig. VI.11. Imports and Exports 1980-81 to 1987-88

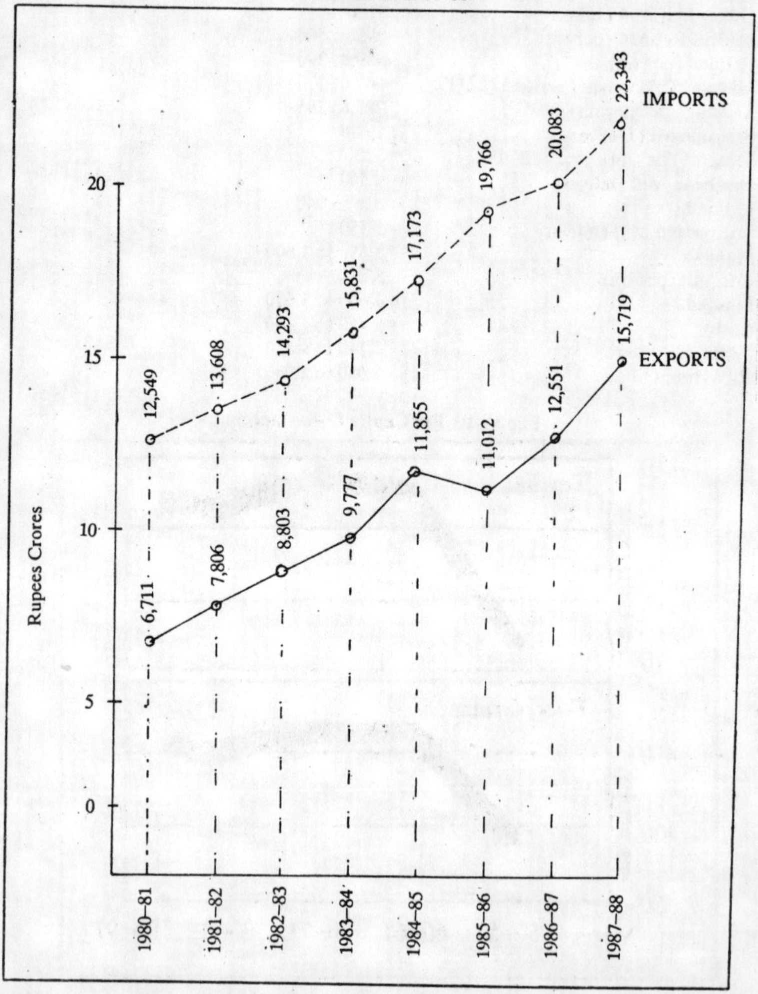

Fig. VI.12. Percentage Exports

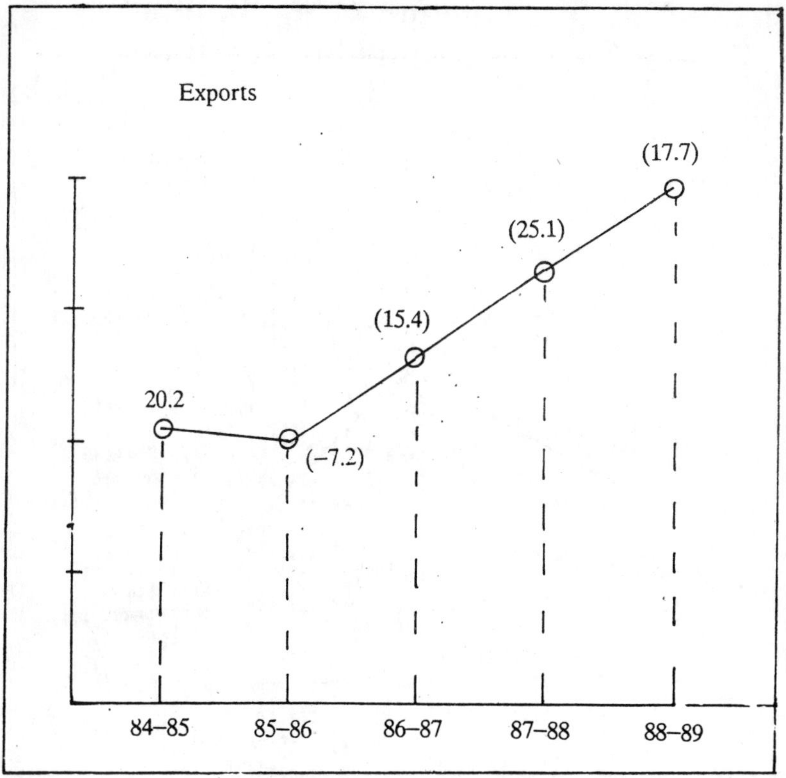

Outstanding Internal and External Debt
(Rs. in crores)

	Outstanding at the end of	
	March 1987	March 1988
(i) Internal debt	86312	99520 (RE)
(ii) External debt (at the current rate of exchange)	32312	36670

	March 1987	March 1988
Outstanding debt as a percentage to GDP:		
(i) Internal debt	29.5%	30.6%
(ii) External debt	11.0%	11.3%

(*Source*: Minister of Finance, L.S., Uns., Q. 1247 , dated 18-11-88)

Fig. VI.13. Indian Exports of Principal Commodities (1987-88)

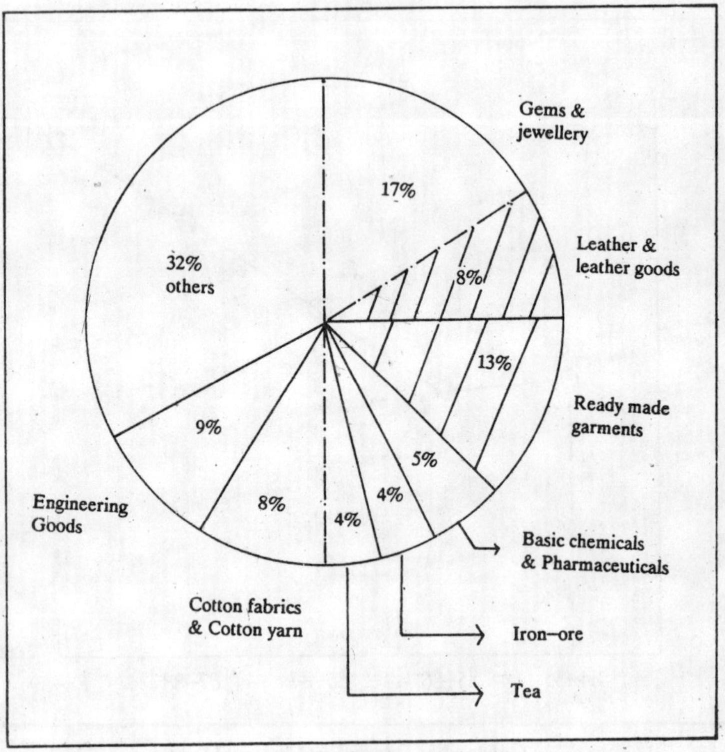

Foreign Exchange Reserve

March 31, 1987	= Rs. 7,645 crores
March 31, 1988	= Rs. 7,287 crores
Oct. 30, 1988	= Rs. 6,352 crores

Black Money

According to a study conducted by the National Institute of Public Finance and Policy, the quantum of black money for 1983-84 was estimated between Rs. 31,584 and Rs. 36,786 crore.

Fig. VI.14. Overall Budgetary Position: Central Government (1950-51 to 1988-89)

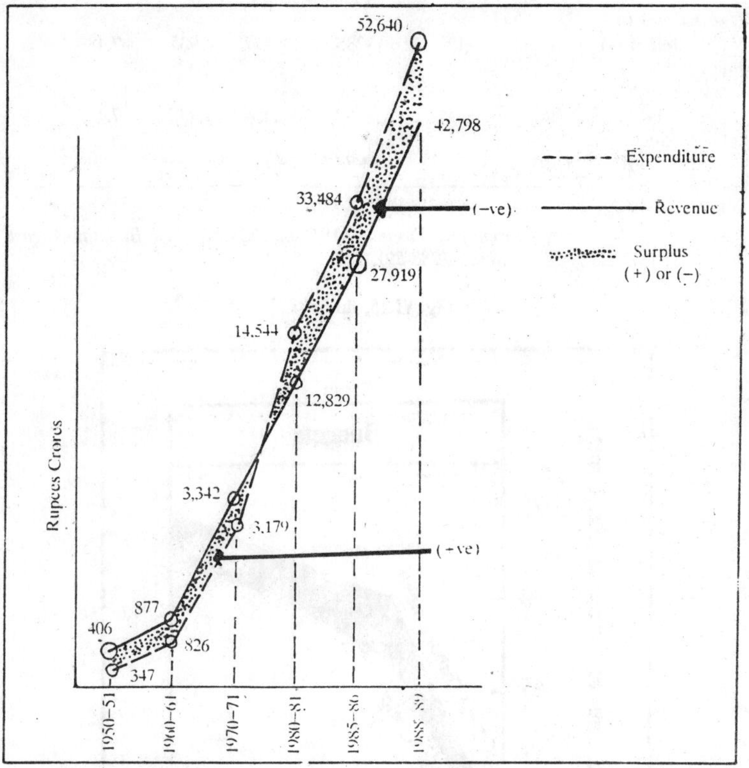

Overall Budgetary Position: Central Government

(Rs. crores)

Item	1950-51	1960-61	1970-71	1980-81	1985-86	1988-89
Revenue account						
(i) Revenue	406	877	3,342	12,829	27,919	42,798
(ii) Expenditure	347	826	3,179	14,544	33,484	52,640
(iii) Surplus (+) or deficit (-)	+59	+51	+163	-1,715	-5,565	-9,842
Capital account						
(i) Receipts	104	1,127	2,524	9,432	16,763	22,278
(ii) Disbursements	182	1,000	2,972	10,294	16,135	20,920
(iii) Surplus (+) deficit (-)	-78	+127	-448	-862	+628	+2,358

Miscellaneous (net)	+15	-61	—	—	—	—
Over surplus (+) or deficit (-)	-4	+117	-285	2,577	-4,937	-7,483
Financed by:						
Treasury bills [increase (-)]	-16	+141	-359	2,754	-4,937	7,484
Cash balances [Decrease (-)]	+12	-24	+74	+177	—	—

(*Source: Report on Currency & Finance, 1965-66,1983-84; RBI Bulletin August, 1985: Budget documents, 1988-89*).

Fig. VI.15. Budgets

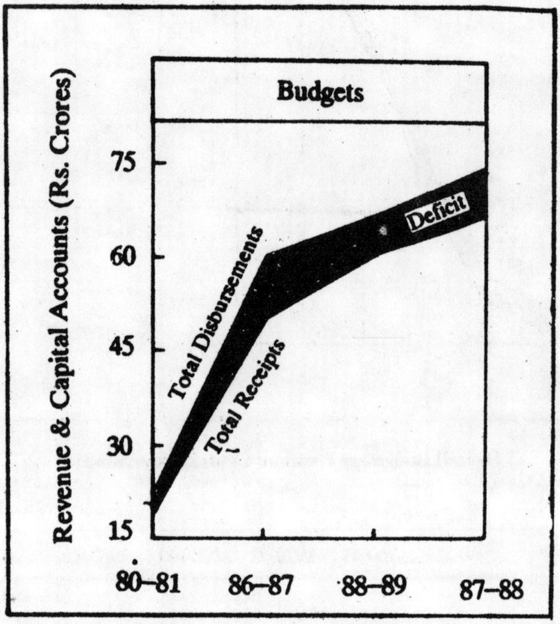

(***Source: Tata Statistical Outline,*** **1988–89**

Fig. VI.16. Defence Overview

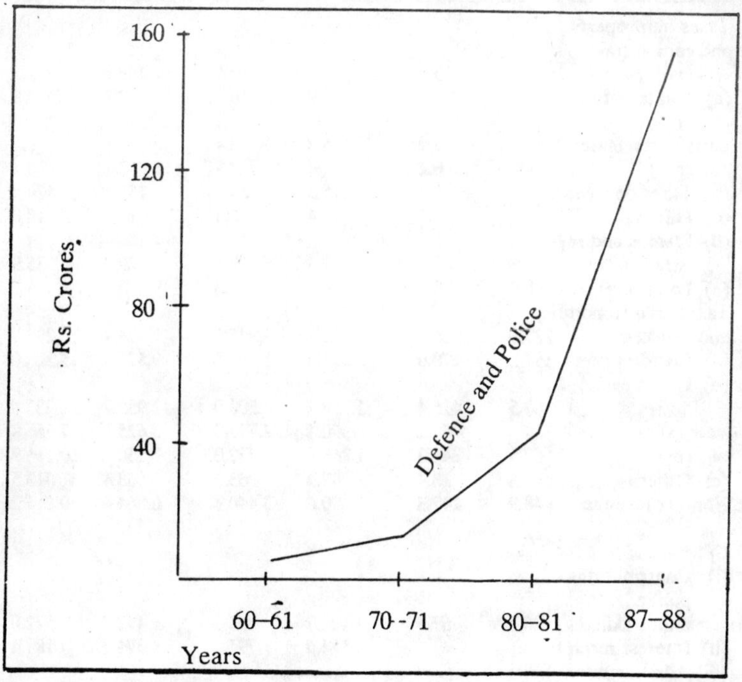

(*Source: CMIE,* 1988)

Revenue Receipts of the Central Government

(Rs. crores)

Head of revenue	1950-51	1960-61	1970-71	1980-81	1985-86	1988-89
Total to revenue	357.0	730.1	2,451.3	9,387.8	21,199.3	31,351.8
Taxes on income and expenditure	125.7	192.0	484.6	1,907.7	3,586.0	4,882.9
(a) Taxes on income, other than corporation tax	132.7	167.4	473.2	1,506.4	2,509.6	3,650.0
Less: states share	47.5	87.4	359.1	1,002.0	1,846.4	2,687.1
(net)	85.2	80.0	114.1	504.4	663.2	782.9
(b) Corporation tax	40.5	111.0	370.5	1,310.8	2,865.1	4,050.0
(c) Others	-	1.0	-	89.5	57.7	50.0

Head of revenue	1950-51	1960-61	1970-71	1980-81	1985-86	1988-89
Taxes on property and capital transactions	3.8	13.5	26.8	87.6	188.9	169.2
(a) Estate duty	-	3.1	7.9	16.3	22.2	3.3
Less: states share	-	2.9	6.3	12.4	18.8	0.2
(net)	-	0.2	1.6	3.9	3.4	3.1
(b) Taxes on wealth	-	8.1	15.3	67.4	153.4	120.0
(c) Gift tax	-	0.9	2.4	6.5	11.7	10.0
(d) Stamps and registration	1.8	3.7	7.5	9.5	20.2	35.9
(e) Land revenue	2.0	0.6	-	0.3	0.2	0.2
Taxes on commodities and services	227.5	524.7	1,939.9	7,395.5	17,424.4	26,299.7
(a) Customs (net)	157.2	170.0	524.0	3,409.3	9,525.8	15,320.0
(b) Union excise duties	67.5	416.4	1,758.6	6,500.0	12,955.7	17,933.0
states share	-	75.1	390.1	2,777.0	5,625.5	7,766.8
(net)	67.5	341.3	1,368.5	3,723.0	7,330.2	10,166.2
(c) Others	2.8	13.4	47.4	263.2	568.4	813.5
Non-tax revenue	48.9	147.3	890.6	3,440.8	6,864.4	10,316.2
Of which:						
(i) Contributions of public undertakings	23.2	53.0	120.7	291.8	472.7	572.0
(ii) Interest receipts			574.6	1,794.6	4,594.7	7,187.4
(iii) Administrative receipts/general services	12.5	59.3	169.7	462.8	1,307.8	2,453.7
(iv) Other revenue	13.2	35.0	25.6	891.6	489.2	103.1
Total revenue	405.9	877.4	3,341.9	12,484.0	28,063.9	41,668.0

Source: *Report on Currency & Finance, 1959-60, 1983-84. RBI,Bulletin, August 1985; Budget documents, 1988-89.*

Unemployment

The number of educated job seekers on the live register of employment exchanges rose from 1,39,75,516 in 1985 to 1,67,35,362 in 1987. West Bengal topped with 23,27,366.

Following table shows the employment situation over the Year 1951 to 1987

Employment Exchange Statistics

Year	Number of employment exchanges at the end of the period	Number of vacancies notified ('000)	Number of registrations during the period ('000)	Number of placements effected ('000)	Number of applicants on the live register at the end of the period ('000)
1951	126	486	1,375	417	329
1956	143	297	1,670	190	758
1961	325	708	3,230	404	1,833
1966	397	852	3,871	507	2,622
1971	437	814	5,130	507	5,100
1976	517	700	5,619	497	9,784
1981	581	750	6,277	504	17,838
1983	638	896	6,756	487	21,953
1985	720	674	5,820	384	24,861
1986	728	623	5,532	348	28,262
1987*	753	453 [a]	4,568 [a]	247 [a]	30,254

(*Source:* *1. Indian Labour Statistics, 1979; Monthly abstract of Statistics, January, 1987.*)

* Figures relate to the month of September, 1987.

a Upto September 1987 only.

CHAPTER 7

AGRICULTURE AND RURAL DEVELOPMENT

Agriculture is the nucleus of almost all activities - it provides food and occupation to majority of India's millions and is the prime source of raw materials for industries. More than a third of India's exports are derived directly from agriculture. It collectively contributes 40 per cent of the net national product.

Indian agriculture, about half a century ago was synonym for famines and poor peasantry. The transformation of the country from almost perpetually out with a begging bowl into the position of an exported is the most illustrious success story of human endeavour. This change in status has been achieved with the four decades of planning against the backdrop of escalating population graph: from 36 crores in 1951 to around 80 crores in 1989.

Self Sufficiency in Food Grains

About 70 per cent of the country's present population of 800 million is dependent on agriculture and it contributess nearly 39 per cent of the gross national product. After the initiation of the First Five Year Plan in 1951, due emphasis on agriculture has been accorded during, the planning process. With the successive Plan periods, foodgrains production as well as agricultural production showed slightly higher growth rates compared to the population increase in spite of the fact that there have been severe droughts, floods and other constraints. During these 38 years of agricultural planning in India, the country has achieved near 'self-sufficiency' in foodgrains from a base level production of 35 million tonnes to a production level of 152 million tonnes and in 1988-89 it is expected to be around 170 million tonnes.

Fig. VII.1. Food Grain Production 1950-51 and 1988-89

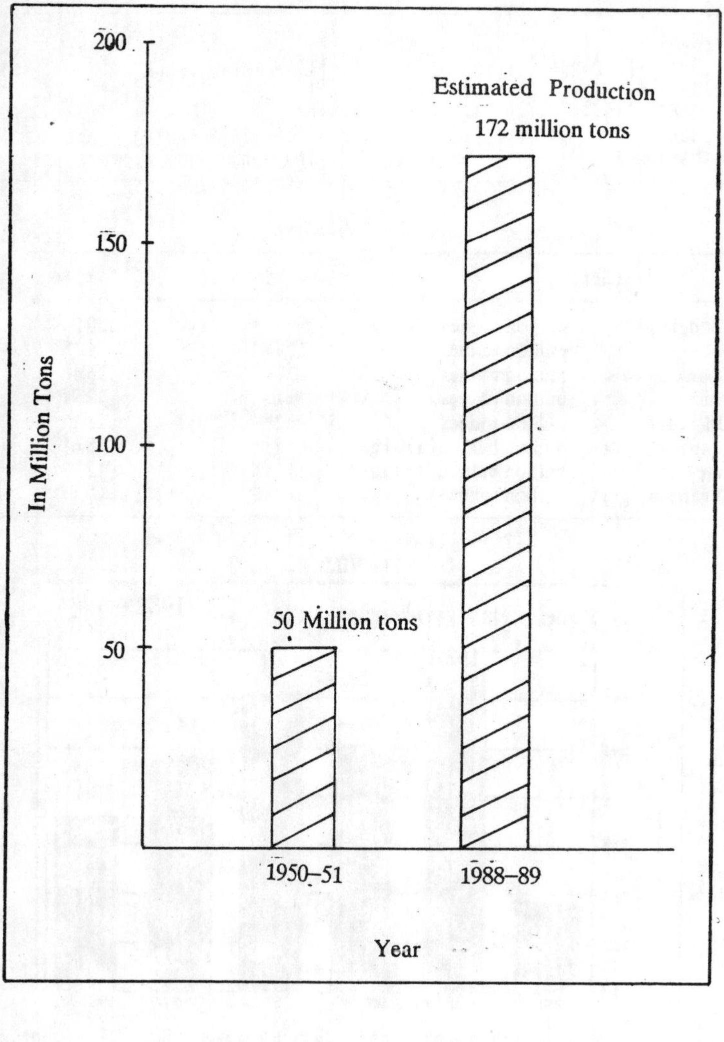

The target for the terminal year of the 7th Plan is 175 million tonnes. Position of food production during the last few years is given below:

Food Production Year	Year ending March Million Tonnes
1984	152.4
1985	145.5
1986	150.4
1987	144.1
1988	138.0
1988-89	172.0 (estimated)

Agricultural Production

	Unit	1949-50	1985-86
Foodgrains	million tonnes	54.92	150.06
Rice	million tonnes	23.54	64.15
Coarse cereals	million tonnes	16.83	26.46
Pulses	million tonnes	8.16	12.97
Oilseeds	million tonnes	5.23	11.15
Cotton	million bales of 170 kg.	2.75	8.61
Jute and mesta	million bales of 180 kg.	3.11	12.73
Sugarcane (gur)	million tonnes	5.02	17.17

Fig. VII.2

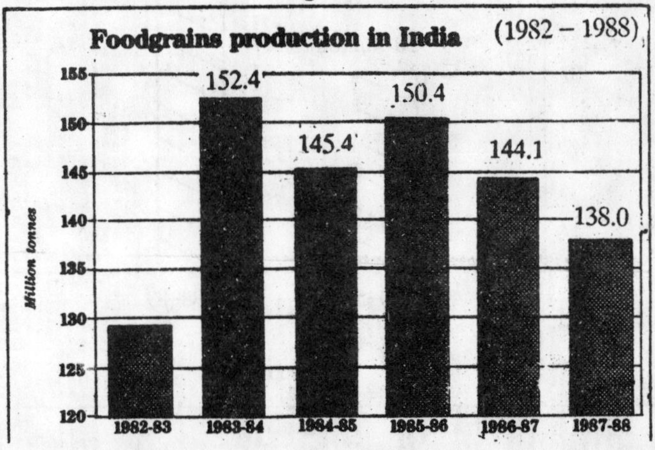

The average rate of growth in foodgrains production has been about 2.5 per cent between 1949-50 and 1986-87. There was a quantum jump in foodgrains production by 17.7 per cent to 152.4 million tonnes in 1983-84. But since then production has declined and due to drought has touched a low of 138 million tonnes in 1987-88. However, due to a good monsoon foodgrains production in 1988-89 is expected to touch in all time high of 172 million tonnes.
(*Source: Business India,* November 28 — December 11, 1987)

Fig. VII.3

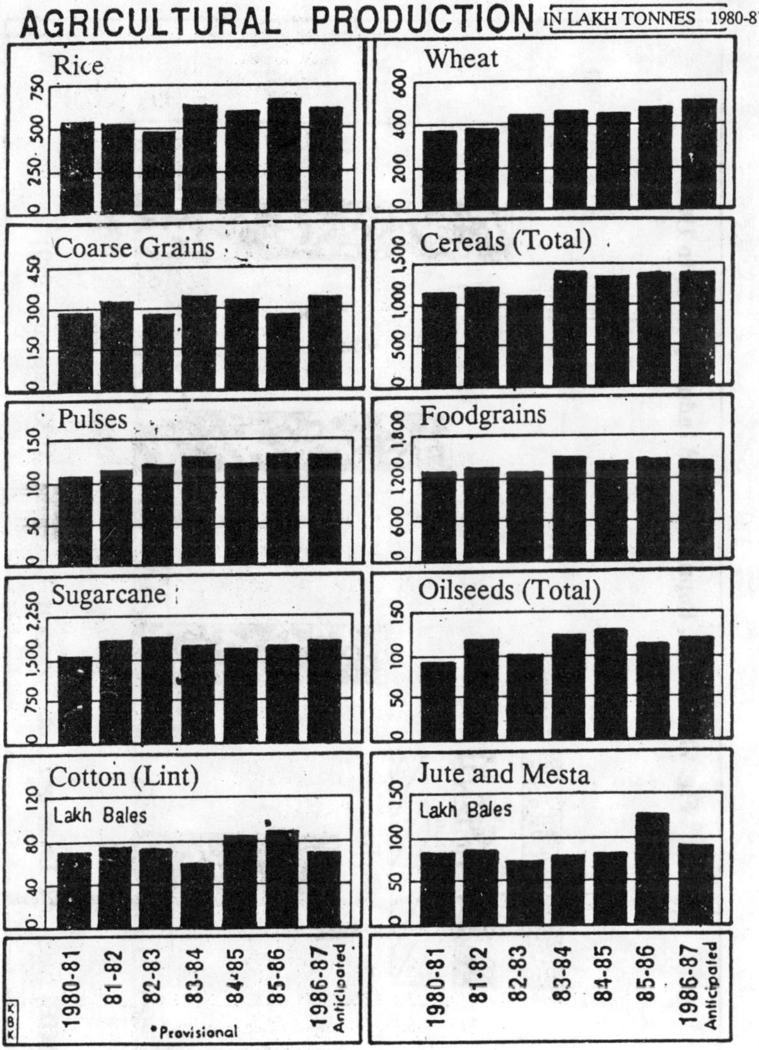

Source: (India 1987)

Oil Production

The production of edible oils during 1989-89 was expected to be about 45 lakh million tonnes against an estimated demand of about 58 million tonnes.

Fig. VII.4. Food, Population and Industry (1950 to 1986)

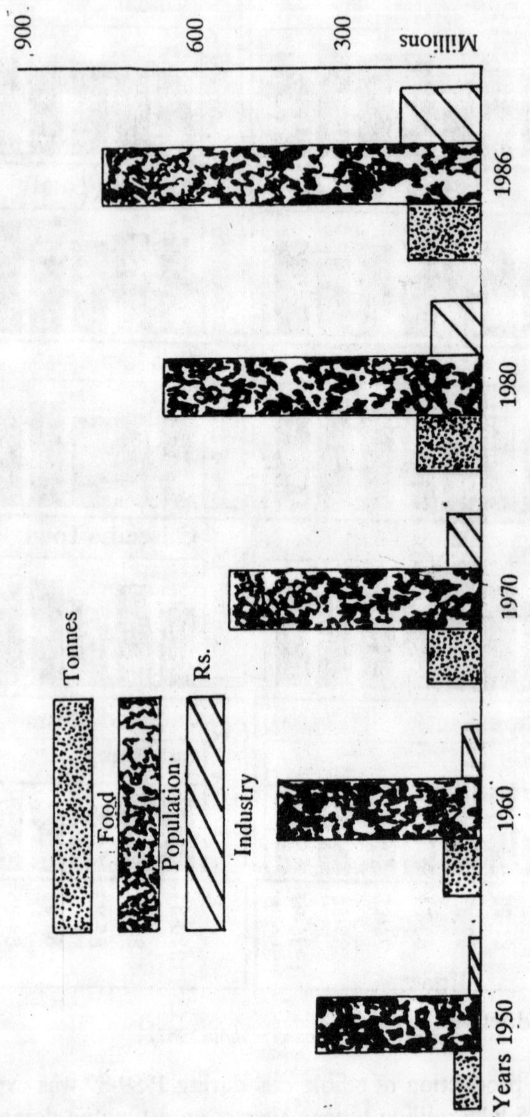

(*Source*: CMIE, 1988 *The Times of India: Economy*, December 1988–January 1989)

Statewise cotton production

	1988-89	1987-88	Change over 1987-88 (in lakh bale)
Punjab	20.00	20.55	- 0.55
Haryana	8.00	8.81	- 0.81
Rajasthan	7.50	4.12	+ 3.38
Gujarat	18.00	4.82	+ 13.18
Maharashtra	18.50	13.33	+ 4.17
Madhya Pradesh	7.00	10.80	- 3.80
Andhra Pradesh	16.00	14.90	+ 1.10
Karnataka	7.00	6.83	+ 0.17
Tamil Nadu	5.25	5.83	- 0.58
Others	0.75	0.75	-
Total all India	108.00	90.74	+ 17.26

The notable increase in production is in Gujarat, where the crop failed last year and to some extent in Maharashtra.

According to the Cotton Advisory Board, of the estimated production of 108 lakh bales for 1988-89 season, about 7.20 lakh bale (7 %) is likely to be short staple, 48 lakh bales (44 %) in medium staple and 52.80 lakh bales (49 %) in long and extra-long staples.

Estimated supply and demand position

	1988	1987-88 (in lakh bales)
Supply		
Carry over with mills, trade and State agencies on September 1	15	20
Production	108	90
Imports	1	3
Total supply	124	113
Demand		
Mills consumption	95	92
Extra factory consumption	5.50	5.50
Exports	5.50	0.43*
Balance carry over on August 31	18	15.05**

* of which Bengal Deshi 5,000 bales

** rounded to 15 lakh bales

Production of Pulses

The requirement and production in 1985-86 were 14.9 and 12.5 million tonnes respectively. The target for 1986-87 was 14 million tonnes, but the production remained at the same level. The target for 1989-90 is 16 million tonnes, but this seems difficult to meet as production has fallen by 15 per cent in 1987-88 due to drought.

Because of shortage, the per capita availability of pulses has gradually declined from 70 gms in 1956 to 38.9 gms in 1985 in the main pulse growing states (Madhya Pradesh, Rajasthan and UP) against the norm of 80 gms recommended by the WHO/FAO. This quantity is sufficiently short of the per capita requirement recommended in the revised ICMR 1981 balance diet.

Crop Yield Per Hectare

(kgs per hectare)

Crops	1950-51	1960-61	1970-71	1980-81	1985-86	1986-87
Rice	668	1013	1123	1346	1552	1482
Wheat	663	851	1307	1630	2046	1998
Jowar	353	533	446	660	633	667
Maize	547	926	1279	1159	1146	1270
Bajra	288	286	622	458	344	401
Pulses	441	539	524	473	547	508
Oilseed	481	507	579	532	570	613
Cotton	88	125	106	152	197	169

Fertilisers

The consumption of fertilisers in 1988-89 is estimated at 10.30 million tonnes as against 8.6 million tonnes in 1987-88.

The Consumption of Chemical fertilisers rose about 4 tonnes during the period 1970-71 to 1986-87.

The following table shows the off-take of fertilisers since 1970-71.

Fig. VII.5. Foodgrains Yield Per Hectare (Kg.): 1985

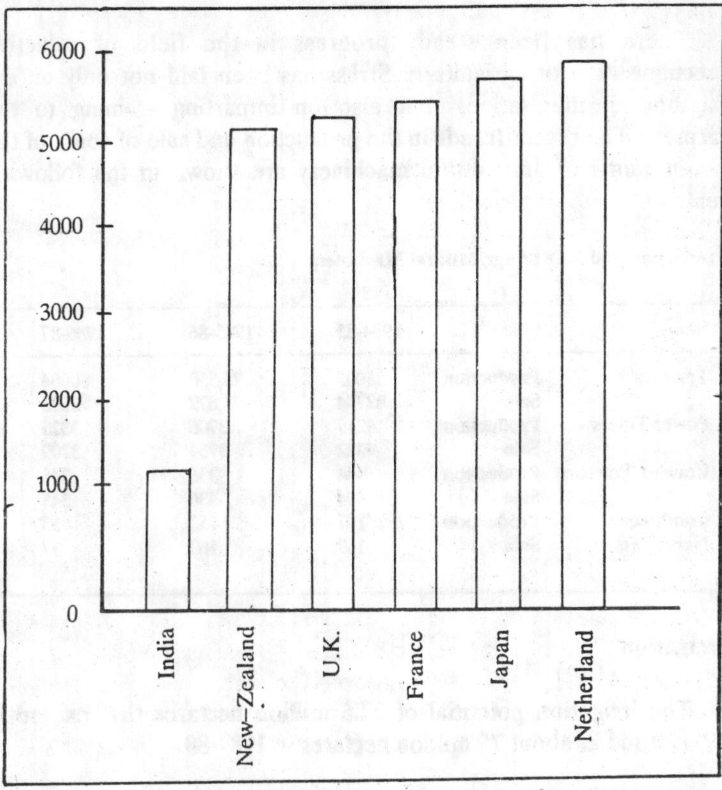

The per hectare yield in foodgrains production has increased from 566 kg in 1949-50 to 1,377 kg in 1985. Even though this is more than 100 per cent increase, India yield rates are low by world standards. There are also glaring disparities in yield rates within India. Punjab has a yield of about 3,000 kg. while Rajasthan has only about 650 kg.

(*Source: Business India*, November 28 December 11, 1987)

Off-take of Fertilisers

(Lakh tonne of nutrient)

Year	Nitrogenous	Phosphatic	Potassic	Total NPK
1970-71	14.9	16.4	2.3	33.6
1980-81	36.8	12.1	6.2	55.2
1981-82	40.7	13.2	6.7	60.6
1982-83	42.2	14.4	7.3	63.9
1983-84	52.1	17.3	7.7	77.1
1984-85	54.9	18.8	8.4	82.1
1985-86	58.2	20.7	8.5	87.4
1986-87	57.7	21.1	8.6	87.4
1987-88 (target)	59.3	22.6	9.2	91.1

Agricultural Machinery

There has been steady progress in the field of selective mechanisation of agriculture. Stress has been laid not only on expanding mechanisation, but also on imparting training to the farmers. The recent trends in the production and sale of some of the major items of agricultural machinery are shown in the following table.

Production and Sale of Agricultural Machinery

Items		1984-85	1985-86	1986-87
1. Tractors	Production	85005	75,550	80004
	Sale	82754	74,879	78823
2. Power Tillers	Production	4219	3706	3325
	Sale	4222	3754	3209
3. Crawler Tractors	Production	444	336	345
	Sale	444	336	345
4. Combine Harvesters	Production	191	153	57
	Sale	167	163	57

Irrigation

The irrigation potential of 22.6 million hectares that existed is 1951, stood at about 75 million hectares in 1987-88.

Irrigation Potential and its Utilisation

(Million hectares)

Year	Major & Medium Schemes		Minor Schemes		All Schemes	
	Potential	Utilisation	Potential	Utilisation	Potential	Utilisation
1980-81	27.3	22.7	31.4	31.4	58.7	54.1
1981-82	28.2	23.2	32.8	32.8	61.0	56.0
1982-83	29.1	24.0	34.2	34.2	63.3	58.1
1983-84	30.0	24.6	35.6	34.0	65.6	58.6
1984-85	30.0	25.3	37.5	35.3	67.5	60.5
1985-86	30.6	25.8	39.2	36.4	69.8	62.2
1986-87	31.2	26.4	40.8	37.7	72.0	64.2
1987-88	31.9	27.0	42.4	39.1	74.3	75.0

Support Prices

The support prices of paddy, coarse cereals, pulses, oilseeds and cotton were announced in Parliament on May 4. It varied from Rs.10 a quintal for paddy and coarse grains to as much as Rs.60 a quintal for sunflower seed and a particular type of cotton. The price rise for pulses was Rs.35 a quintal and for groundnut Rs.40 a quintal. The statutory minimum price of yellow soyabeen was raised by Rs. 20 a quintal and that of black soyabean by Rs. 15 a quintal. In the case of cotton, the increase ranged from Rs. 50–60 a quintal, depending upon the quality and staple length.

Rural Development

Rural development programme has passed through several phases. The first one began with the inception of the Community Development Programme. It was launched on October 2, 1952 with the primary objective of bringing about an overall development in rural India covering cultural and economic aspect of the community life. It sought to achieve the fullest development of available human and material resources on an area basis and thereby raise the rural community to higher levels of living with an active participation of the people themselves. The highest priority in the programmes was given to agriculture.

Initially, a community development block covered an area of about 1,300 sq. km with about 300 villages and a population of 0.2 million. The pattern was revised in 1958 when a block was made to cover 620 sq. km only with 110 villages and a population of about 92,000 persons. Supply of fund for the blocks remained primarily the responsibility of the Central Government till the end of 1966 after which the programme was transferred to the state sector of the plan.

The Government of India has launched a number of schemes for rural development:-

1. Desert Development Programme (DDP)
2. Development of Women and Children in Rural Areas (DWCRA)
3 Drought Areas Programme (DRAP)

4. Integrated Rural Development Programme (IRDP)
5. Minimum Needs Programme (MNP)
6. National Rural Employment Programme (NREP)
7. Rural Landless Employment Guarantee Programme (RLEGP)
8. Training Rural Youth for Self Employment (TRYSEM)

Fig. VII.6

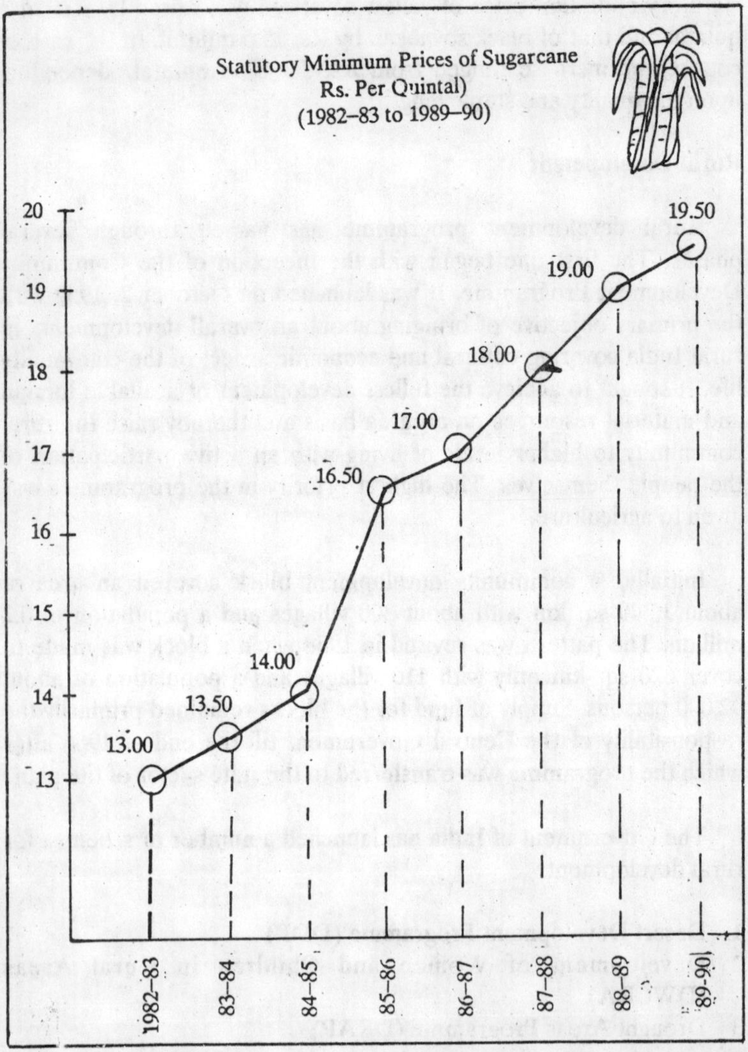

Employment Opportunities in the Rural Areas

An analysis made by the Ministry of Programme Implementation indicates that annual employment created by NREP/RLEGP during 1986-87 and 1987-88 was approximately 2.5 million standard persons per annum. In addition, around 3.7 to 4.2 million families received benefits in the self-employment schemes of IRDP during 1986-87 and 1987-88. This information was given by the Union Minister for Planning and Programme Implementation, Shri Madhavsinh Solanki, while addressing the Members of the Parliamentary Consultative Committee attached to the Ministries of Planning and Programme Implementation in New Delhi recently. Shri Solanki said that the analysis also shows that the village and small industries sector contributed additional employment of the order of 3 million persons during 1985-86. He, however, added that although the contribution in generating rural employment by these programmes would not appear to be substantial in the context of macro demand-supply gap of employment in the country, their importance cannot be minimised in meeting the requirements of the rural poor.

The Minister said that in the field of employment, the major objective of the Seventh Plan has been to ensure that the growth of employment opportunities is faster than the growth in the labour force. It is envisaged that over the Plan period (1985-90), employment potential is expected to increase by 40 million standard person years against an addition to the labour force of 39 million persons.

Forest Policy

The Government of India announced a new forest policy on December 6, 1988. The new policy aims at maintaining environmental stability through preservation and restoration of ecological balance and protecting the remaining forests from further depredation.

Farm Labourers

The number of agricultural labourers in the country as per the latest census carried out in 1981 was 55.5 million. This indicated an increase of 176 per cent as compared to 1951.

New Policy for Importing High Quality Seeds[1]

The Ministry of Agriculture has formulated a New Seed Policy which seeks to secure for the farmer high quality seeds available anywhere in the world to maximise his yields and increase productivity and farm incomes. The Policy came into effect from October 1, 1988.

The new Policy takes further the strategy of the Planning Commission, at the behest of the Prime Minister, to organise cropping patterns suitable for each agro-climatic zone. The variety of these zones confers the advantage of not only growing crops throughout the year but also of producing seeds of crops which thrive in temperate, sub-tropical and tropical latitudes.

The new Policy will facilitate availability of the best high-yielding seeds of different crops suitable for different agro-climatic zones.

A breakthrough in seed technology in pulses being of paramount importance, the New Seed Policy will pay special attention to give farmers access to high quality seeds of pulses. Similarly the key to productivity in coarse grains lies in genetic upgradation.

The New Seed Policy, therefore, focuses on providing the best available seed material from abroad for oilseeds, pulses and coarse grains.

Under the new Policy, import of seeds of vegetables, flowers, ornamental plants, tubers and bulbs of flowers, cuttings and saplings of flowers, etc. will be allowed on OGL through identified categories of importers like the Departments of Agriculture/Horticulture of States, Agricultural Universities, seed producing companies, etc.

The Policy will help crop diversification. It will specially benefit rural areas near metropolitan cities and also those areas where agricultural development has taken place and the accent is now on crop diversification.

---

1. *(Source: Yojana*, October 16-31, 1988)

Vegetables, flowers and fruits have tremendous export potential. The Policy will, therefore, encourage and accelerate production and export on a competitive basis of vegetables and flowers of international standard to increase export earnings.

Significant incentives will also be provided to the domestic seed industry to encourage and promote its growth to meet internal requirements and also to cater to export markets.

CHAPTER 8

INDUSTRIES

Industrial Growth

According to the Annual Report of the Department of Industrial Development for 1987-88 the industrial growth during the eight month of 1987-88 (April–November 1987) was of the order of 10.2 per cent as against 7.5 per cent during the corresponding period last year.

The provisional index of industrial production (Base 1980-81=100) during April-December, 1986-87 increased by 6.8 per cent, mining and quarrying sector showed an increase of 7.3 per cent, electricity generation by 10.3 per cent, food manufacturing by 5.8 per cent, jute, hemp and mesta textile by 7.2 per cent, wood and wood products by 7.6 per cent, paper and paper products by 10.5 per cent, leather and leather products by 3.6 per cent, non-metalic mineral products by 0.6 per cent, chemical and chemical products by 13.4 per cent, basic metal and alloy products by 5.1 per cent, metal products except machinery by 6.2 per cent, machinery and machine tools excepts electric machinery by 6.3 per cent, electric machinery by 14.4 per cent, transport equipment by 5.1 per cent, and other manufacturing industries by 37.5 per cent. However, there had been a decline in output of beverage industries by 5.9 per cent, cotton textile by seven per cent, textile products by 14.5 per cent and rubber, plastic and petroleum products by 1.5 per cent. *(Source: India 1987)*

Coal Production

The coal production in 1988 was estimated to cross 180 million tonnes in 1988 as against 177.4 million tonnes in 1987.

Fig. VIII.1. Index of Industrial Production
BASE 1980-81 = 100

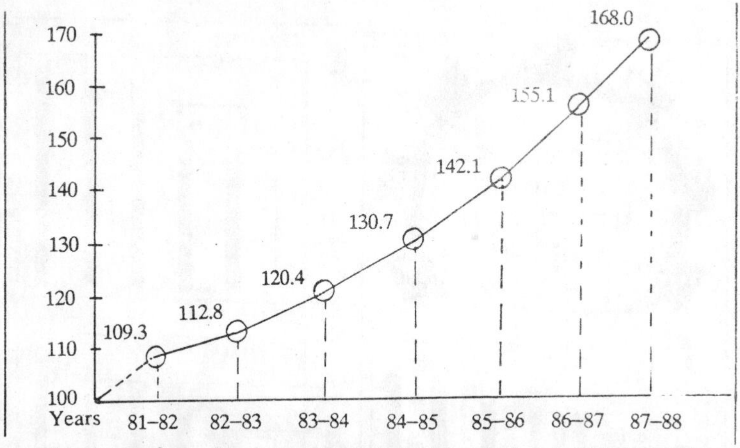

The cost of production which was estimated to be Rs.238.54 per tonne was estimated to be Rs.254 per tonne in 1988-89.

Production of Selected Industries
1982-83 to 1986-87

(Lakh Tonne)

	Cement	Coal	Crude oil	Fertilisers	Ignot Steel
1982-83	234	1305	211	44.04	86.25
1983-84	271	1382.2	260	45.33	79.28
1984-85	302	1474.0	290	51.81	82.96
1985-86	331	1542.4	302	57.56	90.00
1986-87 (Provisional)	364.9	1657.9	304.6	70.70	90.90

(Source: India 1987)

Assets of Ten Large Industrial Houses

S. No.	Name of the Industrial House	Assets (Rs in crores)
1.	Tatas	4,939.88
2.	Birla	4,771.38
3.	Reliance	2,021.53
4.	J.K. Singhania	1,426.67
5.	Thapar	1,151.48
6.	Mafatlal	1,050.50
7.	Modi	860.16
8.	Larsen & Tourbo	830.56
9.	M.A. Chidambaram	807.50
10.	Bajaj	777.79

(Source: Minister of Finance, R.S., S.Q. 117, dated 17-11-1988)

Fig. VIII.2

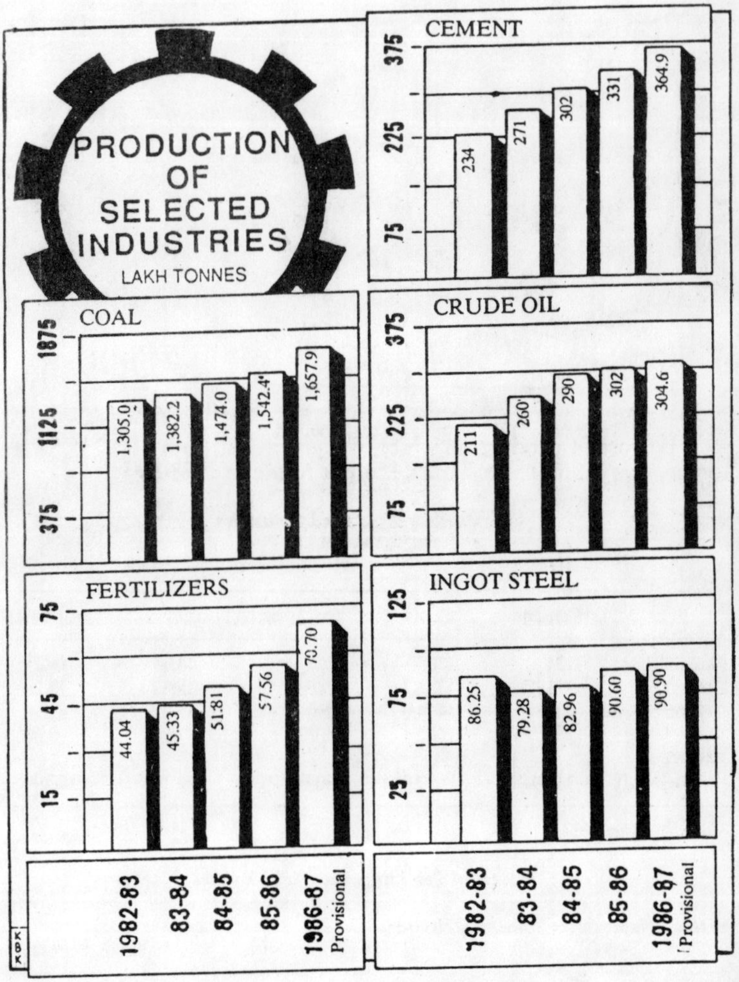

Source: (India 1987)

Fig. VIII.3

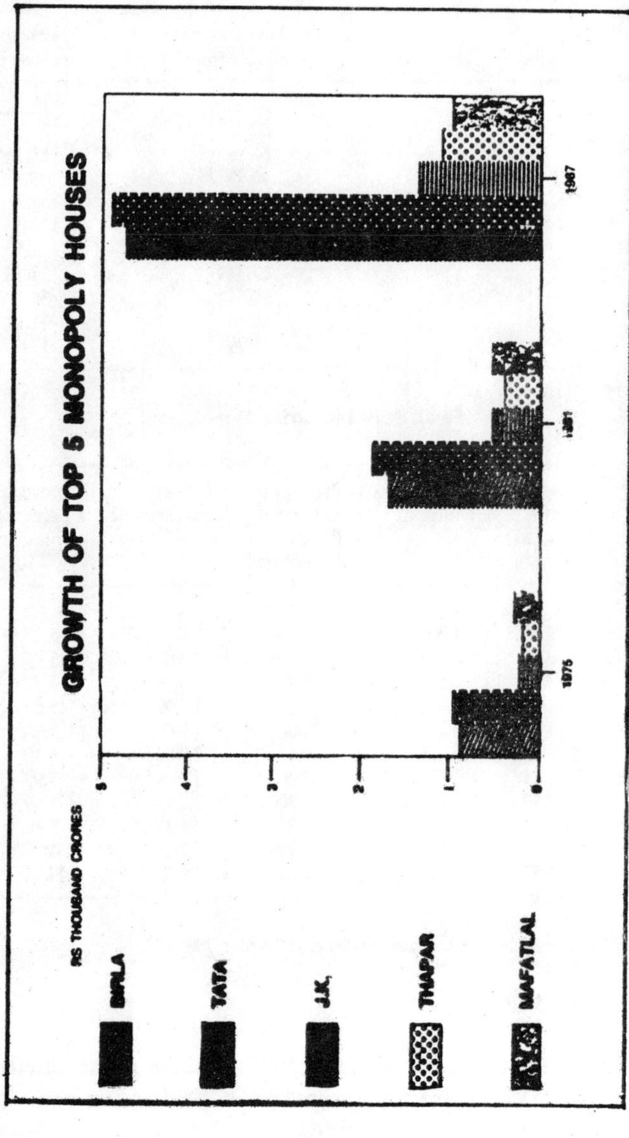

GRAPH COURTESY: INSTITUTE FOR STUDIES IN INDUSTRIAL DEVELOPMENT, NEW DELHI.

Source: (Times of India :Economy Dec. 1988—Jan. 1989)

Top 10 in Computers

	Turnover (Rs. crores)	Growth (1988) (%)
HCL	60.24	32.3
Wipro	54.36	45.7
ECIL	46.49	48.3
ICIM	46.29	-0.2
Sterling	36.04	120.0
DCM DP	23.81	3.5
Hinditron	23.31	32.7
ESPL	20.41	30.7
PSI Data	18.10	31.1
Zenith	15.99	15.0

Small Scale Industries: Growth

Year	No. of units (lakhs)	Employment (million)	Production at current Prices (Rs. crores)	Exports (Rs. crores)	Exports as a percentage of production
1976-77	5.86	5.6	12,400	766	6.17
1977-78	6.63	5.9	14,300	845	5.91
1978-79	7.34	6.4	15,790	1,069	6.77
1979-80	8.05	7.0	21,635	1,226	5.67
1980-81	8.74	7.1	28,060	1,643	5.85
1981-82	9.62	7.5	32,600	2,070	6.35
1982-83	10.55	7.9	35,000	2,095	5.99
1983-84	11.50	8.4	41,300	2,350	5.69
1984-85	12.42	9.0	50,520	2,500	5.10
1985-86	13.53	9.6	61,228	2,785	4.55
1986-87	14.57	10.1	72,250	N.A.	N.A.

(*Source: RBI, Report on Currency & Finance, 1979-86 & 1986-87.*

Khadi Production

Khadi production went up from 104.94 million square metres in 1985-86 to 115.72 square million metres in 1987 and in value from Rs. 195.01 crore to Rs. 227.51 crore.

Fig. VIII.4

Per capita cloth consumption shot up by 33 per cent, from 12.31 metres in 1981 to 16.35 metres in 1987 (the latest year for which fitures are available), and mills have been exporting yarn. Yet the textile industry is still in the doldrums. Even leading mills aren's exactly flourishing, with a few exceptions. Over the last three years, the pre-tax profits of Mafatlal Fine, Morarjee Goculdas, Arving Mills and Lakshmi Mills actually slumped (see chart). Bombay Dyeing and Century Spinning fared better, but they swam against the tide. Clearly, the industry's organised sector was pushed to the background by low-cost powerlooms, which now produce more cloth than the organised sector mills.

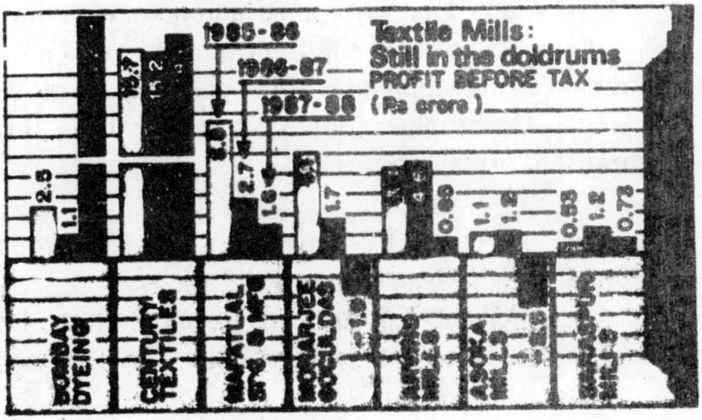

(*Source: India — Today,* January 31, 1989)

CHAPTER 9

EDUCATION

Since 1976, through a constitutional amendment, education has become a joint responsibility of the Central and State Governments. The Department of Education, one of the constituents of Ministry of Human Resource Development looks after education, through the following important organisation:-

1. The University Grants Commission UGC (Co-ordinates and Determines Standards in Higher Education).
2. National Council of Educational Research and Training – NCERT (Strives to promote various aspects of School Education).
3. National Institute of Educational Planning and Administration, New Delhi.
4. Indian Institute of Advanced Study, Shimla.
5. Indian Council of Social Science Research, New Delhi.
6. Indian Council of Historical Research, New Delhi.
7. Indian Council of Philosophical Research, New Delhi.
8. Kendriya Vidyalaya Sangathan, New Delhi.
9. Navodaya Vidyalaya Samiti, New Delhi.
10. Central Board of Secondary Education, New Delhi.
11. Central Institute of Indian Languages, Mysore.
12. Kendriya Hindi Sansthan, Agra.
13. Central Institute of English and Foreign Languages, Hyderabad.
14. Central Hindi Directorate, New Delhi.
15. Commission for Scientific and Technical Terminology, New Delhi.
16. Rashtriya Sanskrit Sansthan, New Delhi.
17. National Book Trust, New Delhi.
18. Indira Gandhi National Open University, New Delhi.

Fig. IX.1. Education Strucure

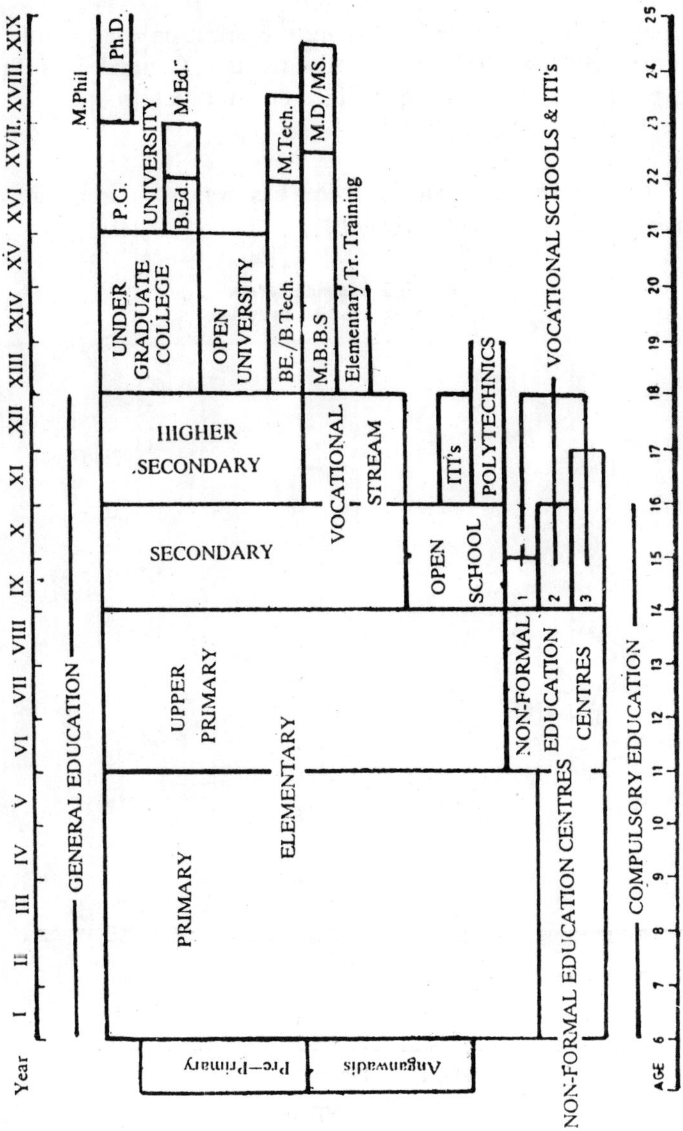

Based on NCERT curriculer, 1986

The major thrust during the year was on implementation of the National Policy on Education 1986.

An amount of Rs. 9693.71 crore was spent on education in the country during 1987-88, jointly by the Central and State Governments. The total expenditure on education from all sources was about Rs. 114 crore in 1950-51.

The period since independence has witnessed a remarkable expansion in all areas of education.

Fig. IX.2. Higher Education
No. of Universities, Instutions

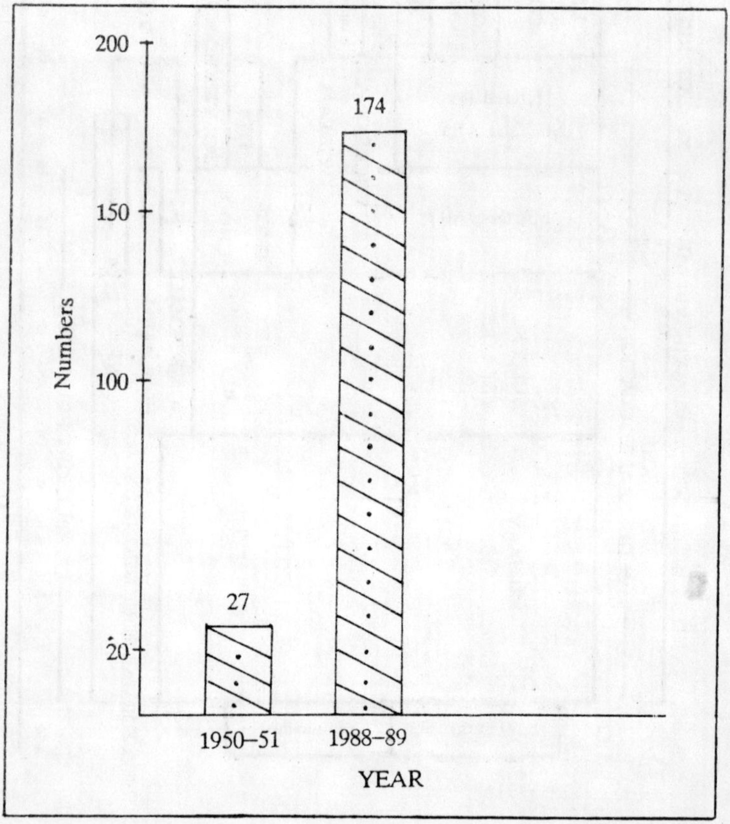

Higher Education

Higher education is imported through 142 Universities, 24 Institutions deemed to be Universities and 10 Institutes of National Importance. At the beginning of the year 1987-88, the total enrolment in Universities and Colleges was 36.82 lakhs. This was 1.11 lakhs more than the enrolment in the previous year.

The number of women students at the beginning of the year 1987-88 was 11.25 lakhs as against 10.59 lakhs in the previous year. The number of teachers increased to 2.35 lakhs during the year.

Fig. IX.3

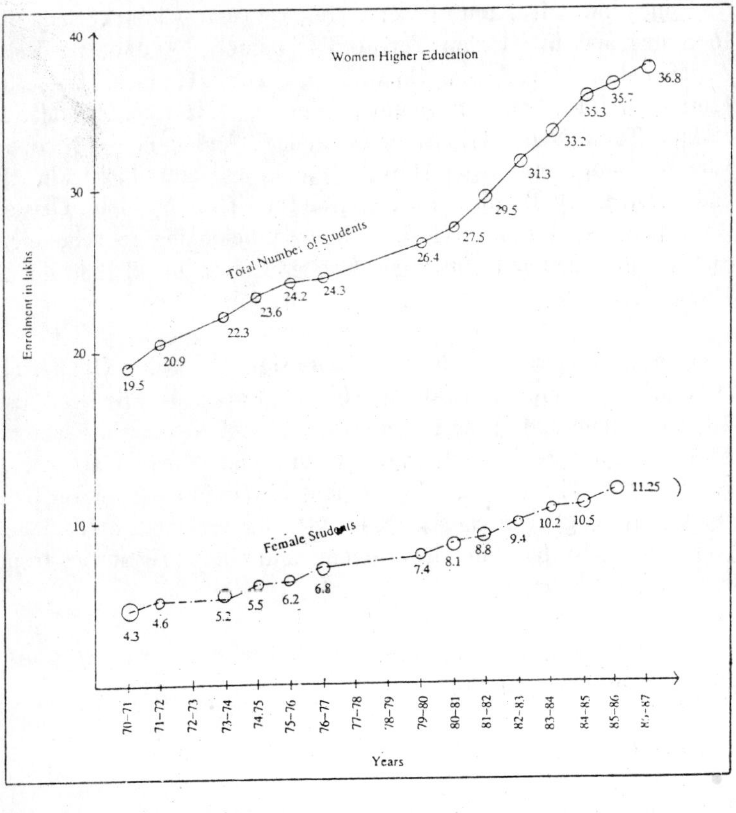

The revised guidelines for the scheme of autonomous colleges was implemented. Till December 1987, 45 Colleges were approved for grant of autonomous status.

New Scales for College Teachers

On July 22, the Government of India announced new pay scales for University and College teachers modifying the earlier pay-scale scheme which had led to wide-spread agitation. The new pay scales of librarians and physical education teachers were also revised.

Secondary Education

Education is free upto lower secondary (upto Class X) stage in 16 States and five Union Territories, namely, Andhra Pradesh, Arunachal Pradesh, Assam, Bihar, Goa, Gujarat, Himachal Pradesh, Jammu and Kashmir, Karnataka, Kerala, Mizoram, Nagaland, Sikkim, Tamil Nadu, Tripura, West Bengal, Andaman and Nicobar Islands, Dadra and Nagar Haveli, Daman and Diu, Lakshadweep and Pondicherry. Besides, it is also free for girls in Manipur, Orissa, Rajasthan and Uttar Pradesh. Children belonging to scheduled castes and scheduled tribes get free education in all States and Union Territories upto Class X.

Education upto the higher secondary state (Class XI-XII) is free in Gujarat, Jammu and Kashmir, Himachal Pradesh, Tripura, West Bengal, Sikkim and in the Union Territories of Arunachal Pradesh, Andaman and Nicobar Islands, Dadra and Nagar Haveli and Pondicherry. The Central Government is reimbursing tuition fees charged from girls in classes IX to XII in government aided/local body schools to the State Governments and Union Territories from the year 1985-86.

The new pattern of education 10+2 has been accepted by almost all States and Union Territories.

Free and Compulsory Education

The target of providing by 1960 free and compuslory education for all children till they reach the age of 14 years as stipulated in Article

45 of the Constitution has been revised from time to time. Now the year 1995 has been fixed as the target year. In spite of rapid expansion, we have been able to enrole about 85% of the children in the age group 6 to 14. But the most important problem is of those students who do not complete primary education. It is estimated that overall national drop out rate of school children from classes I to V is 50.3 per cent. The drop out of children from classes V to VIII is about 25 per cent.

Enrolment Achievements and Targets

(figures in lakh)

	1985-86 Achievements	1986-87 Targets
Agge Group 6-11 Enrolment (Class I-V)	891.26	931.10
Enrolment as per cent of age group population	(95.36)	(99.20)
Age group 11-14 Enrolment (Class VI-VIII)	289.97	312.89
Enrolment as per cent of age group population	(55.63)	(59.76)
Age group 6-14 Enrolment (Class I-VIII)	1,181.23	1,243.99
Enrolment as per cent of age group population	(81.14)	(85.08)

Presently, educatioin in classes I-VIII in all Government/local bodies and aided schools in most of the states/union territories in the country is free.

Operation Black Board

The Scheme of Operation Black Board for brining about substantial improvement in facilities in primary schools is being implemented in a phased manner covering 20 per cent of the blocks and municipal areas in 1987-88, 30 per cent in 1988-89 and 50 per cent in 1989-90 to cover all the primary schools by 1991. A sum of Rs. 100 crore for 1987-88 and Rs. 219.19 crore was earmarked for the scheme. The scheme has three components namely (i) Provision of at least two teachers as far as possible one woman teacher in every primary single teacher school, (ii) Provision of at least two all-weather rooms, and (iii) Provision of essential teaching and learning equipment.

Fig. IX.4. Elementary Education 1950-51 and 1986-87

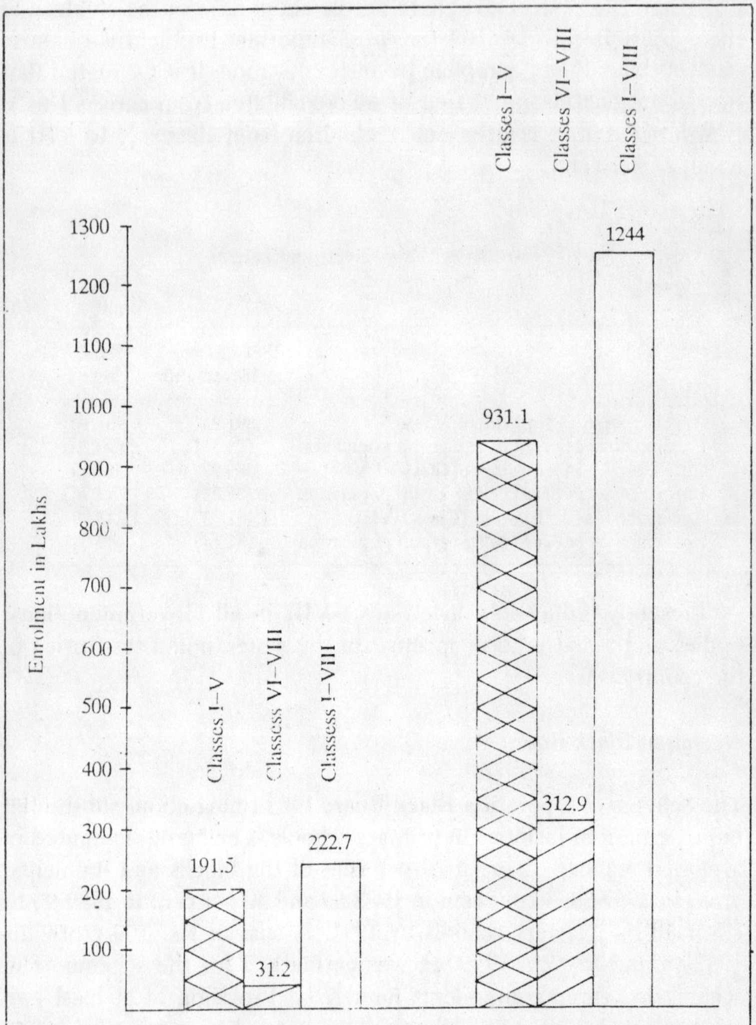

Fig. IX.5. Elementary Education in India
Progress of Enrolment (Lakh Persons)

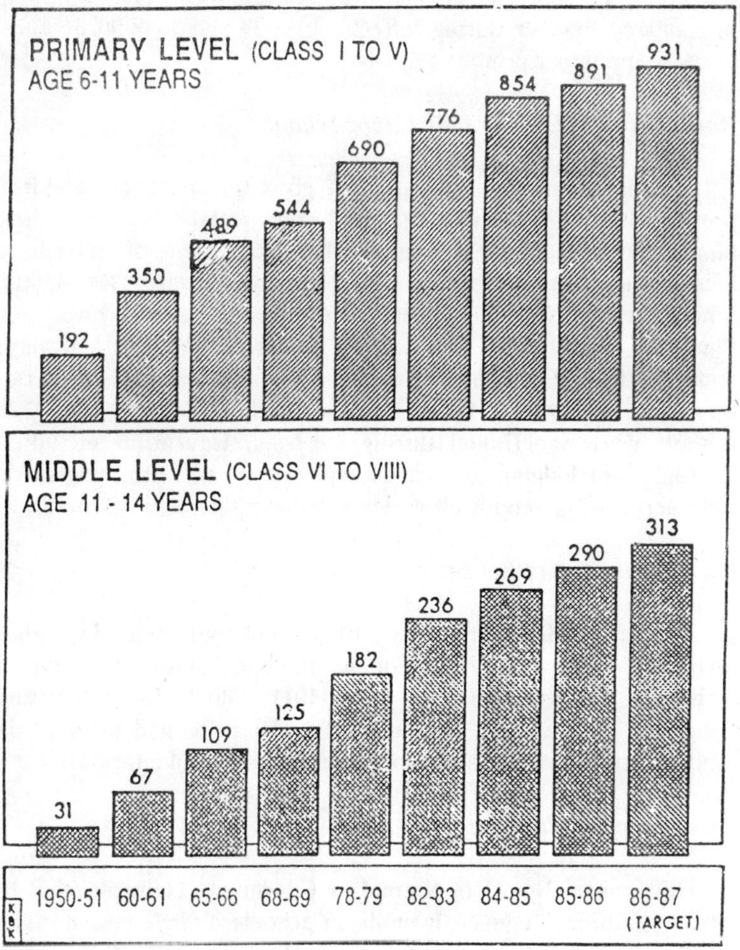

(*Source: India,* 1987).

Qualitative Improvement in Primary Education

With a view to bringing about a qualitative improvement in education, widening access to education and reducing disparities between regions and sections of population, the Ministry of Human Resource Development, initiated a centrally sponsored scheme to distribute one lakh TV sets and five lakh radio-cum-casette players in a phased manner during 1987-88, 1988-89 and 1989-90, to rural primary and upper primary schools.

Navodaya Vidyalayas or Pace Setting Schools

In order to provide education of good quality to the children predominantly (75%) from the rural areas without regard to their family's socio-economic condition, the Government of India have launched a scheme to establish one Navodaya Vidyalya (Residential school) in each district (448 in all) during the Seventh Five Year Plan. An autonomous organisation namely, Navodaya Vidyalaya Samiti with its headquarters in Delhi has been established to run these schools. During 1986-87, 83 such schools were set up. 126 schools were sanctioned during 1987-88. Education including boarding and lodging as well as expenses on uniform, textbooks, stationery etc., is free for all students in these pace setting schools.

Vocationalisation of Education

A target was fixed to diversity 10 per cent students at the higher secondary stage by 1990. For its implementation the Central assistance was sanctioned to cover 1011 schools for conducting vocational courses. An amount of Rs. 50 crore had been made available for the year 1988-89 for vocationalisation of education.

Three Language Formula

The Central Board of Secondary Education, Delhi decided to introduce three language formula in schools affiliated to it. The scheme envisages the teaching of a non-Hindi language, preferably a South Indian language, in schools located in all Hindi speaking States.

Central Board of Secondary Education, Delhi

Since its reconstitution in 1962, the number of schools affiliated to it has increased about 9 times i.e. from 309 in 1962 it went up to

2682 in 1988-89 (as on 31 Dec. 1988). Likewise the number of examinees reached around 3,50,00 from just 16,000. The schools of the Board are located in all parts of the country and 44 schools are abroad. The affiliated schools include all Kendriya Vidyalayas (Central Schools), Military Schools, Schools run by Public Undertakings, Public Schools and Navodaya Vidyalays.

Fig. IX.6. Literacy Rate

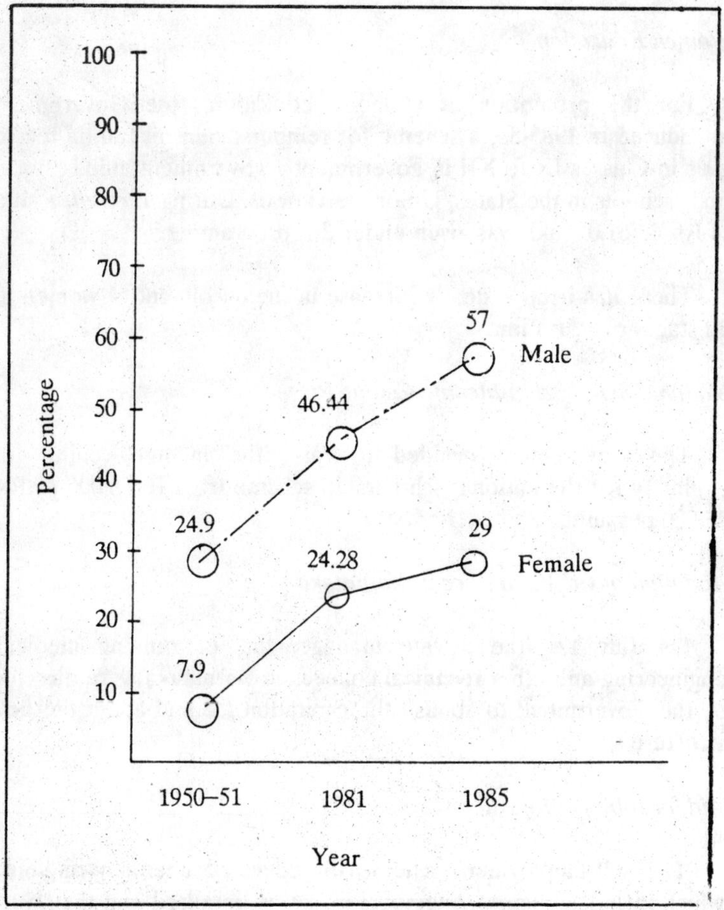

National Literacy Mission

In accordance with the directives of National Policy on Education 1986, the Government launched the National Literacy Mission (NLM) in 1988 in the field of adult education. The objective of NLM is to impart functional literacy to 800 lakh illiterate persons in the age group 15-35 – 300 lakh by 1990 and 500 lakh by 1995. The focus would be on rural areas with a special concern for women and persons belonging to the Scheduled Castes / Scheduled Tribes.

Women Education

For the promotion of women's education, the Government introduced in 1985-86, a scheme for reinbursement of tuition fee to girls in Classes IX to XII in government / government aided / local body schools in the States/Union Territories. During 1986-87, a sum of Rs. 1,361.05 lakh was given under this programme.

There has been a steady increase in the enrolment of women at all stages of education.

National Scholarship Income Ceiling Raised

The Government decided to raise the income ceiling for eligibility for the national scholarship scheme from Rs. 6,000 to Rs. 25,000 per annum.

Abolition of Capitation Fee in Karnataka

On July 12, the private managements of running medical, engineering and other technical colleges in Karnataka were directed by the Government to abolish the capitation fee and adopt the new structure.

Aid for Jobless Professionals

The self-employment scheme for educated unemployed youth which includes doctors, engineers etc., was libralised and they were entitled to get financial assistance to the tune of Rs. 35,000 to undertake self-employment ventures.

Promotion of Education in Border Areas

An amount of Rs. 200 crore has been earmarked for the Seventh Five Year Plan for the promotion of primary education, construction of hostels for middle and secondary schools and residential quarters for teachers. This provision has been made under the Border Area Development Programme on Education for the border States of Gujarat, Rajasthan, Punjab and Jammu and Kashmir.

During 1987-88 Rs. 355.69 lakh was released to Gujarat; Rs. 523.95 lakh to Punjab; Rs. 738.17 lakh to Rajasthan and Rs. 882.19 lakh to Jammu and Kashmir for promotion of education, culture and other youth activities. During the current financial year so far a total amount of Rs. 114.38 lakh has been released to Gujarat (Rs. 30.02 lakh) and Rajasthan (Rs. 84.36 lakh).

Technical Education

Facilities for education and training in engineering and technology have expanded systematically over the past 40 years. During 1988, there were about 180 technical institutions at the first degree level and more than 425 polytechnics at the diploma level with annual admission capacity of 34,000 and 65,000 respectively. More than 80 institutions offer facilities for post-graduate studies and research in engineering and technology with an annual intake capacity of more than 7,000 students. Five national institutions at Bombay, Kanpur, Kharagpur, Madras and New Delhi, known as Indian Institutes of Technology admit about 1,600 students annually. There are 17 regional engineering colleges. Four technical teacher's training institutions located at Calcutta, Bhopal, Chandigarh and Madras provide teachers needed for polytechnics.

Four national level institutes at Ahmedabad, Calcutta, Bangalore and Lucknow with their enrolment capacity of about 500 provide assistance to private and public sector enterprises in meeting their needs for managerial man power.

Educational Statistics
Higher Education

1. No. of Universities Deemed to be	1950-51	1988-89	Increase
Universities and Institutions of National Importance	27	174	App. 7½ times
2. No. of Colleges	695	5,500 (1985-86)	App. 7.9 times
3. Enrolment	3,63,700	(1987-88) 36.82 lakhs	App. 10 times
4. Teachers	18,648	2,35 lakhs (1985-86)	About 12½ times

School Education

Schools	1950-51	1985-86	Increase
(a) High Schools	7288	49,594	App. 7 times
(b) Higher Secondary (Old Pattern)	—	4,511	
(c) Higher Secondary (New Pattern)	—	7,029	
(d) Middle Schools	13,590	1,34,074	About 10 times
(e) Primary Schools	209,671	5,28,079	About 2½ times
(f) Pre-Primary Schools	NA	11,187	

Elementary Education
(1950-51 to 1986-87)

Stage / Classes	Enrolment (1950-51)	Enrolment Estimated 1986-87	Increase
1. Age Group 6-11 Classes I to V.	191.5	931.10	App. 5 times

2. Percentage of Enrolment of total children	42.6	99.2	
3. Age Group 11-14 Classes VI to VIII	31.2	312.9	App. 10 times
4. Percentage of Enrolment	12.7	59.76	
5. Age Group 6-14 Classes I to VIII	222.7	1244.00	App. 11/2 times
6. Percentage of Enrolment in Classes I to VIII	32.3	85.08	

Teachers

Category	Number of Teachers		Increase
	1950-51	1985-86	
1. Primary Schools	5,37,918	15,09,910	About 3 times
2. Middle Schools	85,491	9,67,988	About 11 times
3. High and Higher Secondary	1,26,504	11,58,745	About 9 times
4. Higher Education	18,648	2,26,989	About 12 times
Total	7,68,566	38,63,632	About 5 times

Percentage of Trained Teachers

1.	Primary Schools	58.8%	89.7%
2.	Middle Schools	53.3%	90.3%
3.	High/Secondary Schools	55.5%	91.6%

Percentage of Literacy in India
(1951 to 1985)

Year	Males	Females	Total
1951	24.9	7.9%	16.6
1981	48.89%	24.82%	36.23%
1985	57%	29%	

Litracy Rates for 1971 and 1981

State/Union Territories	1971 Literacy Rates			1981 Literacy Rates		
	Persons	Males	Females	Persons	Males	Females
1	2	3	4	5	6	7
Andhra Pradesh	24.57	33.18	15.75	29.94	39.26	20.39
Assam	28.15	36.68	18.63	N.A.	N.A.	N.A.
Bihar	19.94	30.64	8.72	26.20	38.11	13.62
Gujarat	35.79	46.11	24.75	43.70	54.44	32.30
Haryana	26.89	37.29	14.89	36.14	48.20	22.37
Himachal Pradesh	31.96	43.19	20.23	42.48	53.19	31.46
Jammu & Kashmir	18.58	26.75	9.28	26.69	36.29	15.88
Karnataka	31.52	41.62	20.97	38.46	48.81	27.71
Kerala	60.42	66.62	54.31	70.74	75.26	65.73
Madhya Pradesh	22.14	32.70	10.92	27.87	39.49	15.53
Maharashtra	39.18	51.04	26.43	47.18	58.79	34.79
Manipur	32.91	46.04	19.53	41.35	53.29	29.06
Meghalaya	29.49	34.12	24.56	34.08	37.89	30.08
Nagaland	27.40	35.02	18.65	42.57	50.06	33.89
Orissa	26.18	38.29	13.92	34.23	47.10	21.12
Punjab	33.67	40.38	25.90	40.86	47.16	33.69
Rajasthan	19.07	28.74	8.46	24.38	36.30	11.42
Sikkim	17.74	25.37	8.90	34.05	43.95	22.20
Tamil Nadu	39.46	51.78	26.86	46.76	58.26	34.99
Tripura	30.98	40.20	21.19	42.12	51.70	32.00

Uttar Pradesh	21.70	31.50	10.55	27.16	38.76	14.04
West Bengal	33.20	42.81	22.42	40.94	50.67	30.25
A. & N. Islands	43.59	51.64	31.11	51.56	58.72	42.14
Arunachal Pradesh	11.29	17.82	3.71	20.79	28.94	11.32
Chandigarh	61.56	66.97	54.35	64.79	69.00	59.31
Dadra & N. Haveli	14.97	22.15	7.84	26.67	36.32	16.78
Delhi	55.61	63.71	47.75	61.54	68.40	53.07
Goa, Daman & Diu	44.75	54.31	35.09	56.66	65.59	47.56
Lakshadweep	43.66	56.48	30.56	55.07	65.24	44.65
Mizoram	53.79	60.49	46.71	59.88	64.46	54.91
Pondicherry	46.02	57.29	34.62	55.85	65.84	45.71
INDIA	29.45	39.45	18.69	36.23	46.89	24.82

(*Source: Selected Educational Statistics 1985-86)*

Excludes Assam where census could not be held owing to the disturbed conditions prevailing there at the time of 1981 Census).

According to UNESCO Statistics literacy figures in 1985 for adult males and females were 57 and 29 respectively.

Financial Allocation to Education in Five Year Plans

(Rs. in Crores)

Plan	Total Plan Outlay	Expenditure	Outlay on Education	Expenditure on Education	Per cent of Plan Outlay on Education to Total Plan
First Five Year Plan (1951-56)	2,356	1,960	169	153	7.2
Second Five Year Plan (1956-61)	4,800	4,672	277	273	6.4
Third Five Year Plan (1961-66)	8,209	8,557	560	589	7.3
Annual Plans (1966-69)	6,756	6,625	331	321	4.8
Fourth Five Year Plan (1969-74)	24,882	16,160	822	786	3.5
Fifth Five Year Plan (1974-78)	53,411	42,300	1,285	912	3.3
Sixth Five Year Plan (1980-85)	1,72,210	1,49,750	2,524	2,943	1.5
Seventh Five Year Plan (1985-1990)	180,000	–	5,733	–	–

Plan Outlay and Expenditure on Education

(Rs. in Crores)

Sector	First Plan		Second Plan		Third Plan	
	Outlay	Expenditure	Outlay	Expenditure	Outlay	Expenditure
1	2	3	4	5	6	7
1. Elementary Eductation	93 (55)	85 (56)	93 (34)	95 (35)	209 (37)	201 (34)
2. Secondary Education	22 (13)	20 (13)	49 (18)	51 (19)	88 (15)	103 (18)
3. University Education	15 (9)	14 (9)	47 (17)	48 (18)	82 (15)	87 (15)
4. Other Educational Programmes	16 (9)	14 (9)	33 (12)	27 (9)	29 (5)	66 (11)
5. Cultural Programmes	@	@	4 (1)	3 (1)	10 (2)	7 (1)
6. Total General Education	146 (86)	133 (87)	226 (82)	224 (82)	418 (75)	464 (79)
7. Technical Education	23 (14)	20 (13)	51 (18)	49 (28)	142 (25)	125 (21)
8. Total Education	169 (100)	153 (100)	277 (100)	273 (100)	560 (100)	589 (100)

Note: **Figures in Parenthesis indicate percentage to total.**
@ Included under General Education.

(Contd.)

1966-67 to 1968-69 Annual Plan		Fourth Plan		Fifth Plan		Sixth Plan		Seventh Plan (1985-1990)
Outlay	Expenditure	Outlay	Expenditure	Outlay	Anticipated Expenditure (1974-78)	Outlay	Expenditure	
8	9	10	11	12	13	14	15	16
—	74.7	256	239	410	317	905	870	1963
—	(23.2)	(31)	(30)	(32)	(35)	(36)	(30)	(34)
—	52.6	118	140	250	156	398	743	
—	(16.4)	(14)	(18)	(19)	(17)	(16)	(25)	
—	77.0	183	195	292	205	486	537	2595
—	(24.0)	(22)	(25)	(23)	(22)	(19)	(18)	(45)
—	32.8	127	94	140	99	331	347	
—	(10.2)	(16)	(12)	(11)	(11)	(13)	(12)	
—	3.7	13	12	37	28	104	119	132
—	(1.1)	(2)	(2)	(3)	(3)	(4)	(4)	(2)
—	240.8	697	680	1,129	805	2224	2616	5051
—	(74.9)	(85)	(87)	(88)	(88)	(88)	(89)	(88)
—	80.7	125	106	156	107	300	329	682
—	(25.1)	(15)	(13)	(12)	(12)	(12)	(11)	(12)
331.00	321.5	822	786	1,285	912	2524	2943	5733
—	(100)	(100)	(100)	(100)	(100)	(100)	(100)	(100)

(*Source: A Handbook of Educational and Allied Statistics, Government of India, 1987*)

CHAPTER 10

FISCAL ISSUES

Following are the Comparative figures for the last three years:

1. Central Grants to States

(Rs. in Crores)

	States	1985-86	1986-87	1987-88
1.	Andhra Pradesh	99.07	87.59	95.73
2.	Arunachal Pradesh	—	15.67	119.94
3.	Assam	159.26	183.29	208.08
4.	Bihar	161.77	135.68	150.25
5.	Gujarat	61.28	65.79	64.30
6.	Haryana	48.22	24.18	17.80
7.	Himachal Pradesh	152.89	150.74	207.03
8.	Jammu & Kashmir	109.26	120.46	139.50
9.	Karnataka	61.38	62.47	61.73
10.	Kerala	86.76	83.76	65.67
11.	Madhya Pradesh	95.59	102.81	113.77
12.	Maharashtra	105.36	109.72	105.30
13.	Manipur	89.03	95.37	108.03
14.	Meghalaya	57.93	82.46	97.38
15.	Mizoram	—	8.39	54.62
16.	Nagland	110.98	122.01	143.60
17.	Orissa	60.55	72.32	78.50
18.	Punjab	76.94	16.58	14.57
19.	Rajasthan	67.06	70.98	80.00
20.	Sikkim	40.39	47.22	53.42
21.	Tamil Nadu	97.08	89.27	112.85
22.	Tripura	82.96	96.81	113.06

23.	Uttar Pradesh	304.96	322.27	373.31
24.	West Bengal	66.90	79.78	88.40
25.	Goa	–	–	24.96
	TOTAL	2,195.62	2,246.62	2,601.86

(*Source: Minister of Finance, L.S., Uns. Q. 2124, dated 25-11-88*)

2. Central Transfer to State

Estmated Central Transfer to States in 1989-90

Sl. No.	State	Share of Taxes and Duties Total	Grants (Non-Plan) Total	Total Col (1) +(2)	Percent to Total Col. (3)
1.	Andhra Pradesh	848.70	52.81	901.51	6.60
2.	Arunachal Pradesh	65.30	85.90	151.20	1.11
3.	Assam	404.28	158.52	562.80	4.12
4.	Bihar	1372.99	81.95	1454.94	10.65
5.	Goa	24.59	22.36	46.95	0.34
6.	Gujarat	422.13	14.47	436.50	3.19
7.	Haryana	137.05	27.76	164.81	1.21
8.	Himachal Pradesh	140.46	113.98	254.44	1.86
9.	Jammu & Kashmir	236.44	238.60	475.04	3.48
10.	Karnataka	560.31	15.64	575.95	4.22
11.	Kerala	404.41	6.61	411.02	3.01
12.	Madhya Pradesh	909.56	44.78	954.34	6.98
13.	Maharashtra	860.47	56.50	916.97	6.71
14.	Manipur	75.27	73.62	148.89	1.09
15.	Meghalaya	59.67	52.07	111.74	0.82
16.	Mizoram	72.52	97.97	170.49	1.25
17.	Nagaland	73.38	97.78	171.16	1.25
18.	Orissa	509.55	109.06	618.61	4.53
19.	Punjab	184.22	94.39	278.61	2.04
20.	Rajasthan	574.68	76.62	651.30	4.77
21.	Sikkim	14.06	17.31	31.37	0.23

22. Tamil Nadu	839.36	32.75	872.11	6.38
23. Tripura	97.59	85.42	183.01	1.34
24. Uttar Pradesh	2046.75	116.67	2163.42	15.83
25. West Bengal	851.90	103.34	955.24	6.99
Total (All States)	11785.64	1876.78	13662.42	100.00

3. Excise and Custom Duties[1]

Presently excise and customs duties contribute roughly 80% of the tax revenue of the Centre. In 1948-49 the share of Direct Taxes in the Central Tax Revenue was about 52.7% and the share of indirect taxes about 47.3%. This trend has been reversed over the years. In a developing country with low per capita income it was but natural that more and more dependence was placed in indirect taxes to raise revenue to meet the various plan objectives of the country. Revenue from customs duties has grown from about Rs. 130 crores 1948.49 to an estimated figure over Rs. 15,500 crores in the current year. Likewise revenue from excise duties has grown from about Rs. 51 crores in 1948-49 to an estimate of over Rs. 18,100 crores in the current year. At present excise and customs revenue form about 10% of GDP.

In the case of Customs, the cost of collection as percentage of revenue is about 1.11 while for Central Excise it is about 1.8%.

Customs duties have been levied in one form or other from ancient times. The tariff schedules have been undergoing changes over the years. The schedule contained in the Indian Tariff act 1934 was replaced by a schedule based on the Brussels Tariff Nomenclature in 1976. This tariff schedule was in turn replaced by a Schedule based on the Harmonised System of Nomenclature in 1986. Bulk of the revenue is from machinery, crude oil, chemicals, metals, vegetable oils, plastics and baggage. The Public Sector accounts for about 50% of customs revenue. Specific rated goods contribute about 30% of the total revenue.

----

1. *(Source: (N. Raja - Commissioner (TRU), The Hindustan Times, January 28, 1989)*

Central Excise is the larges single source of central revenue contributing 42.72% of the total revenue. Forty four commodities contribute over 90% of the total revenue. In 1987-88 crude oil contributed 1892 crores, cigarettes 1470 crores, man-made fibre yarn 1535 crores, motor spirit 902 crores, cement 869 crores, motor-vehicles 689 crores, machinery goods 579 crores, iron and steel 630 crores, refined diesel oil 646 crores, tyres and tubes 556 crores, sugar 478 crores. The group-wise growth in respect of the major commodities has shown an increase of 35% for petroleum and oil products with collections at 4090 crores, 10% for textiles (2175 crores), 9% for tobacco products (1691 crores), 8% for transport (1251 crores), 16% for metals (895 crores) and 7.7% for other products (1798 crores).[2]

4. Money and Banking 1987-88

	August 12, 1988	August 28, 1987	Change in 1 year
Currency with the public	35,098	29,681	4,511
Demand deposits with banks	24,574	21,478	3,243
Time deposits with banks	1,13,565	96,993	16,849
Other deposits with RBI	230	215	46
Net bank credit to Govt. Sector	94,720	77,574	16,044
Net bank credit to Comm. sector	1,08,837	95,739	13,099
Foreign exchange assets	3,757	4,453	-841
Scheduled Commercial Banks			
Total credit	72,659	64,306	8,132
Food advances	1,642	4,457	-2,836
Non-food advances	71,017	59,849	10,968
Cash and balances with RBI	21,832	17,380	4,157
Borrowings from RBI	1,035	1,206	-797
Investments	50,908	43,082	7,979

---

2. (*Source*: M.M. Sethi, Member Central Board of Excise and Customs, *The Hindustan Times*, January 28, 1989)

Money and Banking 1970-86

(Rs. Crores)

Item	As on last Friday of: 1970-71	1980-81	1985-86	1986-87
1. Currency with the public	4,367	13,464	25,168	28,539
2. Deposit money of the public	2,954	9,653	18,431	22,457
3. Total (1 + 2) = M_1	7,321	23,117	43,599	50,996
4. Post-Office savings banks deposits	990	2,338	3,047	2,954
5. Total (3 + 4)-M_2	8,311	25,355	46,646	53,950
6. Time deposits with banks	3,637	32,241	74,739	89,260
7. Total (3 + 6) = M_3	10,958	55,358	1,18,338	1,40,256
8. Total post office deposits	1,184	6,512	11,772	11,270
9. Grand total (7 + 8) = M_4	12,142	61,870	1,30,110	1,51,526

(Source: Report on Currency & Finance, 1986-87)

Currency in Circulation and with the Public

(Rs. crores)

Item.	Amount outstanding on the last Friday of						
	1960-61	1970-71	1980-81	1983-84	1984-85	1985-86	1986-87
Notes in circulation	1,946	4,169	13,689	19,888	23,088	25,519	28,762
Circulation of Rupee coins	142	247	333	386	426	531	709
Circulation of small coins	71	137	286	333	351	409	432
Currency in circulation	2,155	4,553	14,308	20,607	23,865	26,459	29,903
Of which: With banks	50	186	844	1,054	1,202	1,291	1,364
Currency with public	2,105	4,367	13,464	19,553	22,663	25,168	28,557

(*Source: Report on Currency & Finance 1969-70 & 1986-87*)

Issue and Mintage of Coins

(Rs. Crores)

Year	Issued		Mintage		Percentage of mintage of small coins to total small coins issued
	Rupee notes & coins (total)	Small coins	Rupee coins	Small coins	
1970-71	248	127	0.1	7.0	5.5
1975-76	336	209	15.6	30.0	14.3
1980-81	348	243	13.8	4.7	1.9
1981-82	366	262	13.9	3.7	1.4
1982-83	377	277	16.5	6.0	2.1
1983-84	401	290	18.6	15.8	5.4
1984-85	441	307	25.8	19.5	6.3
1985-86	546	366	42.7	44.0	12.0
1986-87	724	444	45.8	50.2	11.3

(*Source:* *Report on Currency & Finance 1986-87*)

Money and Prices: Annual Variations[a]

(Per cent)

Year	Monetary resources (M_3)	Index number of: Wholesale prices	Index number of: Consumer prices for industrial workers	Index number of: Consumer prices for agricultural labourers
1970-71	11.2	5.5	5.1	(-) 0.5
1971-72	13.1	5.6	3.2	4.2
1972-73	15.9	10.0	7.8	12.5
1973-74	15.5	20.2	20.8	25.8
1974-75	6.9	25.2	26.8	30.0
1975-76	15.0	(-) 1.3	(-) 1.3	(-) 13.9
1976-77	23.6	2.1	(-) 3.8	(-) 4.7
1977-78	18.4	5.2	7.6	7.0
1978-79	21.9	0.0	2.2	(-) 1.9
1979-80	17.7	17.1	8.8	13.6
1980-81	18.1	18.2	11.4	13.6
1981-82	12.5	9.3	12.5	9.5
1982-83	16.1	2.6	7.8	7.4
1983-84	17.9	9.5	12.6	8.7
1984-85	18.7	7.6	6.4	0.4
1985-86	16.1	3.8	6.5	5.7
1986-87	18.5	5.3	8.7	4.1
Average variation (1970-87)	16.3	8.6	8.4	7.1

(*Source: RBI, Report on Currency and Finance, 1986-87; RBI, Bulletin, August 1985.*

a Annual variations are measured as percentage change over the previous year.

The overdues of the public sector banks went upto Rs. 10,972 crore at the end of December 1987 as against of Rs. 7214 crore at the end of December 1985.

Fig. X.1

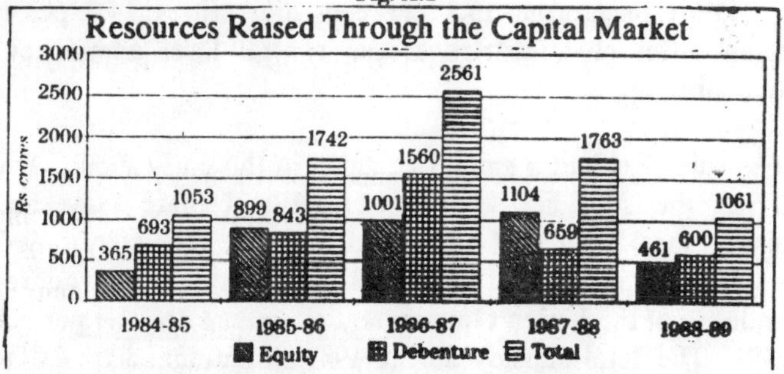

Capital markets are playing an increasing role in resource generation. Resources raised through the capital market (equity and debentures) by non-government public limited companies in 1984-85 was Rs. 1,058 crores, which peaked in 1986-87 (Rs. 2,561 crores), and has again declined to around Rs. 1,763 crores in 1987-88. In 1988-89, it is expected that the amount should cross Rs. 2,000 crores. Debentures remain the favourite and the largest source of resoure generation.
(*Source: Business India*, January 23—February 5, 1989)

The Punjab National Bank topped nationalised banks with regard to deposits and advances (excluding interbank deposits and advances as on September 3, 1988. The bank had deposits worth Rs. 8,924.67 crore and had made advances of Rs. 4,359.1 crore. The other in the top five were Central Bank of India, Bank of India, Canara Bank and Bank of Baroda.

Investment in Joint Ventures Abroad

Year	Value in Rs. Lakhs
1985	312.70
1986	404.35
1987	515.67

(*Source: Minister of Commerce, L.S. Uns. Q. 1289, dated 18-11-1988*)

5. Subsidies for Social Justice

For attaining the objective of social justice, it is necessary that income levels or the purchasing power of the citizens are increased. In case income level cannot be raised alone the poverty line, then it becomes essential to subsides some of the important consumption goods. From this point of view several subsidies have been introduced over the years. The subsidies have a basic accompaniment of the mixed economy. There are 34 different subsidies and of which the fertilizer subsidy and the food subsidy are the major ones. An analysis of different subsidics in 1987-88 budget would indicate that food accounted for 35 per cent, fertilizer 35.2 per cent, export promotion 15.3 per cent and others 14.5 per cent. Thirteen different ministries at the central level administer the various subsidies.

The subsidies had a small beginning in the early 1950's. During 1950-51, the subsidies of the Central and State Governments accounted for 4.3 per cent of Central and State budgets. In 1987-88, the subsidies accounted for 15.2 per cent of the aggregate expenditure of the Union Government as against only 1.7 per cent in 1970-71. The total subsidy during 1987-88 amounted to Rs. 9,350 crore of which the Central Government's commitment was Rs. 5,605 crore.

Estimates of Total Subsidies

(Rs. crores)

Year	Central Government Subsidies	State Government Subsidies	Total (2+3)
1950-51	—	—	41
1960-61	—	—	93
1970-71	94	243	337
1971-72	140	282	422
1972-73	205	346	551
1973-74	361	347	708
1974-75	419	764	1,183
1975-76	470	650	1,120
1976-77	947	446	1,393
1977-78	1,287	485	1,772
1978-79	1,475	726	2,201
1979-80	1,543	699	2,525
1980-81	2,028	927	2,839
1981-82	1,941	1,231	3,172
1982-83	2,262	1,545	3,807
1983-84	2,902	2,208	5,110
1984-85	4,208	2,987	7,195
1985-86	4,929	3,085	8,014
1986-87	5,579(RE)	3,721	9,300
1987-88	5,605(BE)	3,745	9,350

Source: Publications of Centre for Monitoring Indian Economy, Bombay.)

Details of Subsidies by the Central Government 1979-80 to 1987-88

(Rs. crores)

	1979-80	1980-81	1981-82	1982-83	1983-84	1984-85	1985-86	1986-87 (RE)	1987-88 (BE)
A. **Major Subsidies**	1,487	1,554	1,558	1,791	2,339	3,546	4,305	4,681	4,780
1. Food	600	650	700	711	835	1,101	1,650	2,000	2,000
2. Indigenous fertilisers	234	170	281	550	900	1,200	1,600	1,700	1,750
3. Imported fertilisers	283	335	100	53	141	727	450	193	160
4. Export Promotion and Market Development	361	399	477	477	463	518	605	788	870
B. **Other Subsidies**	56	474	383	471	563	662	624	898	825
5. Railways	56	69	78	97	93	100	128	147	178
6. Mill-made cloth	—	76	125	56	53	53	52	36	27
7. Handloom cloth	—	36	52	54	0	0	0	127	127
8. Import/export of sugar, edible oils etc.	—	—	—	8	0	2	108	0	0
9. Interest subsidies	—	253	102	217	390	507	336	313	289
10. Other subsidies	—	40	26	30	27	0	0	275	204*
Total (Subsidies)	1,543	2,028	1,941	2,262	2,902	4,208	4,929	5,579	5,605

* Includes Rs. 24 crore, subsidy for white printing paper for education purpose.

(*Source: Publications of Centre for Indian Economy, Bombay.*)

CHAPTER 11

DIVERSE ISSUES

1. Child Labour

The evil of child labour is both large and wide-spread in India in spite of the enactment of the 1939 legislation relating to the abolition of child labour. About 18 million children work in the country to earn bread for their families. The unofficial sources place the figure between 44 million and 100 million.

Fig. XI.1. Villages El.ctrified at on 31-3-1988 — All India

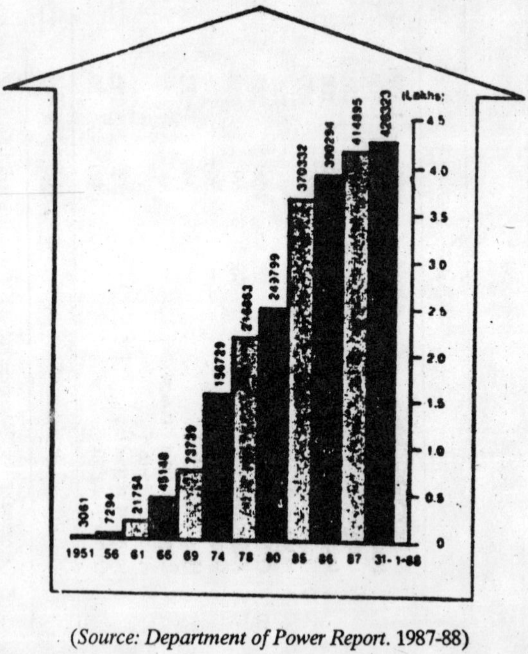

(*Source: Department of Power Report*. 1987-88)

Fig. XI.2

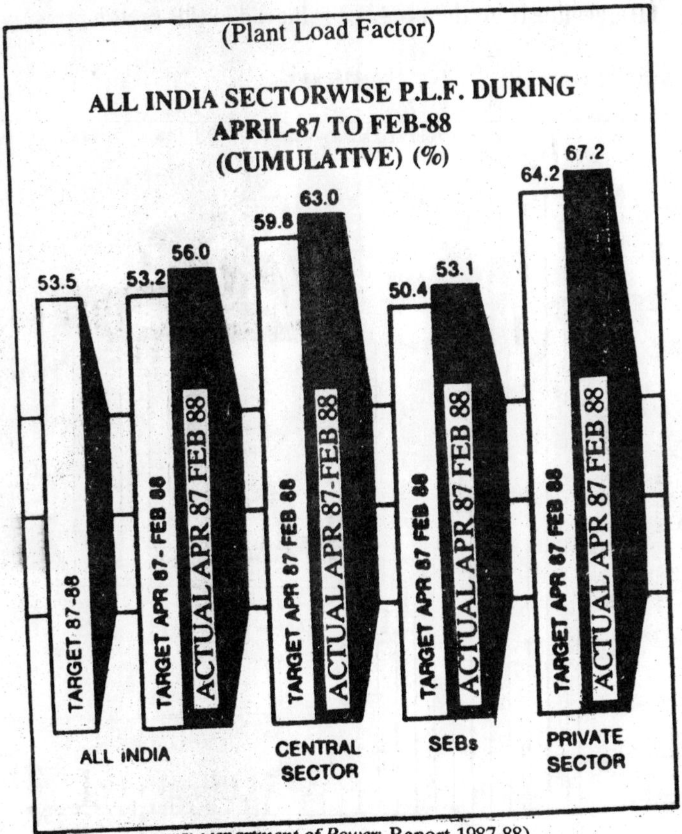

(*Source: Department of Power*: Report 1987-88)

Work may prolong from 4 a.m. to 12 p.m. as is found in many hotels or in cottage industries. Children as small as 3 years are employed at the Sivakasi match Factories in Tamil Nadu. Carpet, weaving, bidi-rolling, match and fire work factories, glass bangle and potterly industries all employ and exploit children.

2. Energy Conservation

Enery is going to be a major challenge in the years ahead. A number of steps have been taken to increase the generation. The load factors are to-day at the highest that have ever been since independence.

Graphs illustrate the progress achieved in this sector.

Fig. XI.3

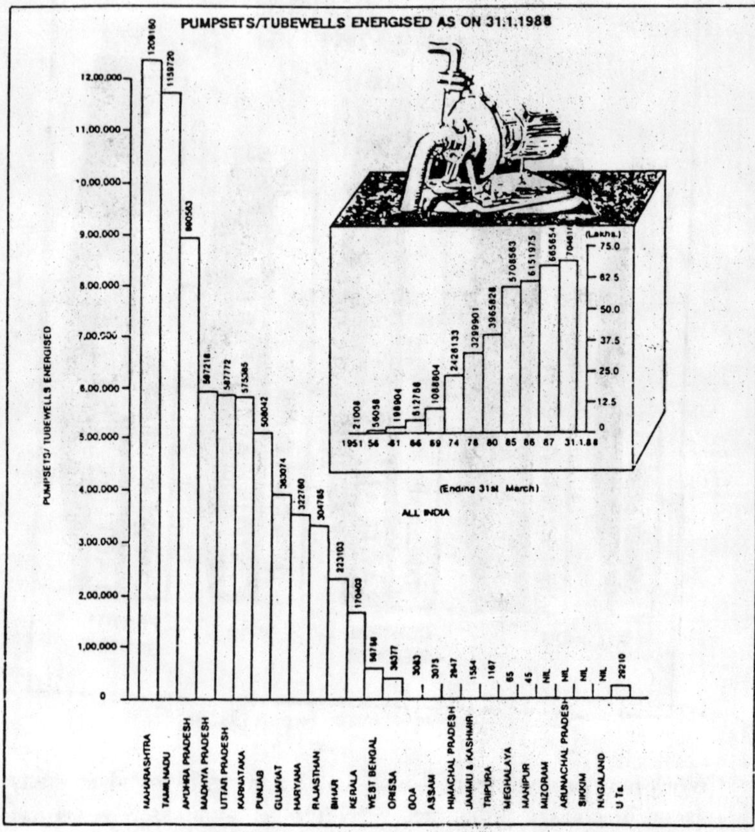

Source (Department of Power: Report 1987-88

3. Health and Nutrition

1. % of Infants with low birth weight-1982-87 30%
2. % of children five suffering in 1980-85 from:

	(a) Mild-moderate malnutrition	33%
	(b) Severe malnutrition	5%
3.	Daily per capita calorie supply as % of requirements 1985	94%
4.	Percentage fully Immunized 1986-87 (One year old children)	
	TB	46%
	DPT	58%
	POLIO	50%
	Measles	17%
	Pregnant women-tetnus	47%
5.	ORS per 100 episodes of diarrhoea (Litres) 1986	18
6.	% of Births attended by trained health personnel 1983-87	33%
7.	Maternal mortality rate 1980-87 per 100,000 live births	500
8.	% of population with access to drinking water 1980-87	
	(a) Urban	80%
	(b) Rural	47%
	Total	56%
9.	% of Household income spent on All Food 1980-85	52%
10.	One doctor for	3,620 persons

4. Mass Media

T.V. Facilities

The TV service was available to about 75 per cent of the country's population in 1988.

T.V. Tower

The 235 metre high T.V. Tower, reportedly the highest in Asia, was commissioned by the Prime Minister in Delhi on 7.11.88. It is at thrice the height of Qutab.

Film Export

Indian film exports earned the country Rs. 7.30 crore during

1987-88 with Hindi titles contributing the largest share of Rs. 6.06 crore.

No. of Films

Indian film production slumped in 1986 compared to the boon years between 1973 and 1985. As compared with 913 films in 1985, 840 films were produced in 1986.

Thematic Classification of Films Certified in 1986

Classification	Number
Social	601
Crime	137
Others	28
Devotional	17
Fantasy	15
Mythological	13
Historical	7
Legendary	6
Horror	4
Stunt	4
Biographical	3
Children's film	2
Children's/legendary	1
Social/fantasy	1
Social/legendary	1
Total	840

(*Source: Journal of the Film Chamber, February, 1987.*)

Number of Cinemas

Year	Number of Cinemas
1978-79	9,960
1979-80	10,562
1980-81	10,813
1981-82	11,239
1985-86	12,680
1987-88	16,000 (Estimated)

Radio

The total number of transmitters is 170 covering 98% of total population and 79.81% of the total area. The number of radio sets per 1000 persons is 66.

Television

The total number of TV transmitters is now 255 covering 75% of the total population. The number of Television sets per 1000 person is five.

News papers

As many as 27,685 newspapers and periodicals were registered with the Registrar of Newspapers of India as on December 1987.

Following are the figures of a newspapers per person 1984.

Country	No. of daily Newspapers	Circulation (in 1,000s)	People per Newspapers
Japan	125	67,380	1.8
USSR	724	116,096	2.4
UK	108	23,206	2.4
Hong Kong	67	NA	3.3
Australia	62	4,588	3.4
Singapore	10	700	3.6
USA	1,687	63,263	3.7
Canada	112	5,544	4.5
South Korea	14	5,906	6.9
Malaysia	40	1,670	9.1
Thailand	25	NA	21
Philippines	22	2,022	26
China	60	30,000	35
India	1,334	14,847	50
Indonesia	55	2,878	57

(*Source: UNESCO Statistical Year Book 1987*).

News paper Wage Board

On August 30, 1988, the Wage Board headed by Justice U.N. Bachawat announced its tentative proposals for wage revision of journalists and non-journalists employees in newspapers and news agencies. Newspapers were categorised into ten categories and news agencies into six on the basis of gross revenue.

Telephones

The 37,223 villages in the country had been connected by telephone upto September 30, 1988.

During the years (1985-88), a total of 9,04 lakh new telephone connection were provided in the country.

5. Public Sector

The investment in the public sector grew from Rs. 49 crore in 1951 to over Rs. 61,000 crore by 1986.

Fig. XI.4 Public Sector in India

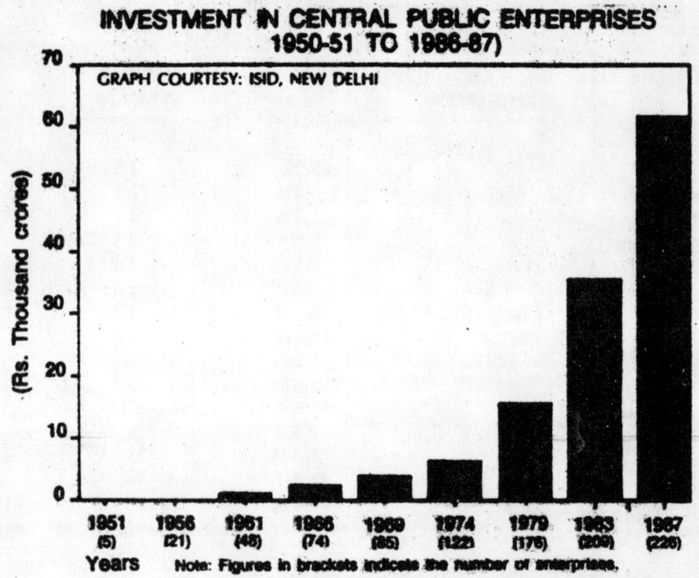

Source: (Times of India: Economy Dec. 1988-Jan, 1989)

6. Railways

Growth and Progress

Item	1950-51	1960-61	1970-71	1980-81	1984-85	1985-86	1986-87
Route kilometres	53,396	56,247	59,790	61,240	61,850	61,836	61,813
Electrified route kms:	388	748	3,706	5,345	6,325	6,517	7,275
Locomotive (No.).							
Steam	8,120	10,312	9,387	7,469	5,970	5,571	4,950
Diesel	17	181	1,69	2,403	2,905	3,047	3,182
Electric	72	131	602	1,036	1,253	1,302	1,366
Coaches ('000)	13	20	25	27	28	28	28
Wagons (''000)	206	308	384	401	365	360	354
Railways stations (No.)	5,976	6,523	7,066	7,035	7,093	7,092	7,105
No. of employees ('000)	914	1,157	1,374	1,572	1,603	1,613	1,612
Cost of staff (Rs. crores)	114	205	460	1,317	2,353	2,707	3,332
Av. cost per employee (Rs.)	1,263	1,799	3,398	8,435	14,797	16,883	20,862
Passenger Traffic:							
Originating (Mn.)	1,284	1,594	2,431	3,613	3,333	3,433	3,580
Kilometers (Mn.)	66,517	77,665	1,18,120	2,08,558	2,26,582	2,40,614	2,56,468
Earnings (Rs. crores)	98.2	131.6	295.6	827.5	1,456.8	1,719.4	1,939.7
Av. fare per passenger km (paise)	1.48	1.71	2.50	3.97	6.43	7.15	7.56
Goods Traffic:							
Freight originating (Mn. tonnes)	93.0	156.2	196.5	220.0	264.8	286.4	307.3
Fright tonnes kms (Mn.)	44,117	87,680	1,27,358	1,58,474	1,82,161	2,05,904	2,23,097
Earnings (Rs. crores)	139.3	280.5	600.7	1,550.9	3,465.0	4,232.2	4,990.7
Average rate per tonne km (paise)	3.16	3.87	54.3	10.50	20.10	21.50	23.30

(*Source: Indian Railways, Annual Report & Accounts, 1986-87*).

Financial Position of Indian Railways

(Rs. crores)

Item	1950-51	1960-61	1970-71	1980-81	1985-86	1986-87
Capital at charge	827.0	1,520.9	3,330.3	6,096.3	9,078.1	10,373.1
Total Investment	855.2	1,868.6	4,099.4	7,448.4	11,492.0	13,306.9
Revenue—gross receipts	263.3	460.4	1,007.0	2,703.5	6,590.7	7,683.1
Working expenses, including depreciation etc.	215.7	372.6	862.2	2,576.0	5,904.8	7,002.2
Net revenue receipts	47.6	87.9	144.8	127.5	685.9	680.9
% of net revenue receipts to capital at charge	5.8	5.8	4.4	2.1	7.6	6.6
Operating ratio (per cent)	81.0	78.8	84.1	96.1	90.6	92.2
Dividend to general revenues	32.5	55.9	164.6	325.4	507.0	578.9
Surplus/deficit (-)	15.0	32.0	(-) 197.8	(-) 197.9	178.8	102.0

(*Source: Indian Railways, Annual Report & Accounts, 1986-87*).

Utilisation Capacity of Railways

	Net tonne-kms per tonne wagon capacity per annum (in terms of 4 wheeler)		Passenger kms. per 1000 seating capacity (in million)	
	BG	MG	BG	MG
1960-61	16,558	10,125	61.2	44.4
1965-66	15,567	12,255	65.4	47.6
1970-71	15,117	12,583	71.2	52.8
1975-76	16,412	12,313	80.1	57.9
1980-81	16,285	11,013	105.2	71.0
1981-82	18,366	12,227	112.7	72.4
1982-83	18,455	13,091	114.4	75.7
1983-84	18,349	13,068	110.3	70.7
1984-85	18,942	12,567	106.1	73.7
1985-86	21,165	15,206	111.3	78.3
1986-87	23,211	15,878	118.0	84.1

Source: *Indian Railways Year Book, 1986-87)*
Note: BG. Broad guge & MG: Medium gauge.

7. Science and Technology

Free India is determined to catch up with the contemporary technological revolution. India made significant progress during 1988 in fields such as space and nuclear energy oceanography and metallurgy, bio-technology and industrial and defence electronics. India has put satellites into orbit and built its own launch vehicles to do so. During 1988, India became the fifth nation to have its remote sensing satellite. The other four nations are the United States, the Soviet Union, France and Japan.

The bulk of the research effort in India is financed by major scientific agencies such as the Departments of Science and Technology, Atomic Energy, Space, Scientific and Industrial Research, Electronics, Non-Conventional Energy Resources, Environments, Ocean Developments, Biotechnology and Indian Council of Medical Research etc. There are about 200 research laboratories within the purview of these major scientific agencies carrying out research in different areas. Besides, there are a large number of scientific institutions under the Central Ministries/ Departments which carry out research programmes of practical relevance to their areas of responsibility.

Fig. XI.5 Finances of Indian Railway

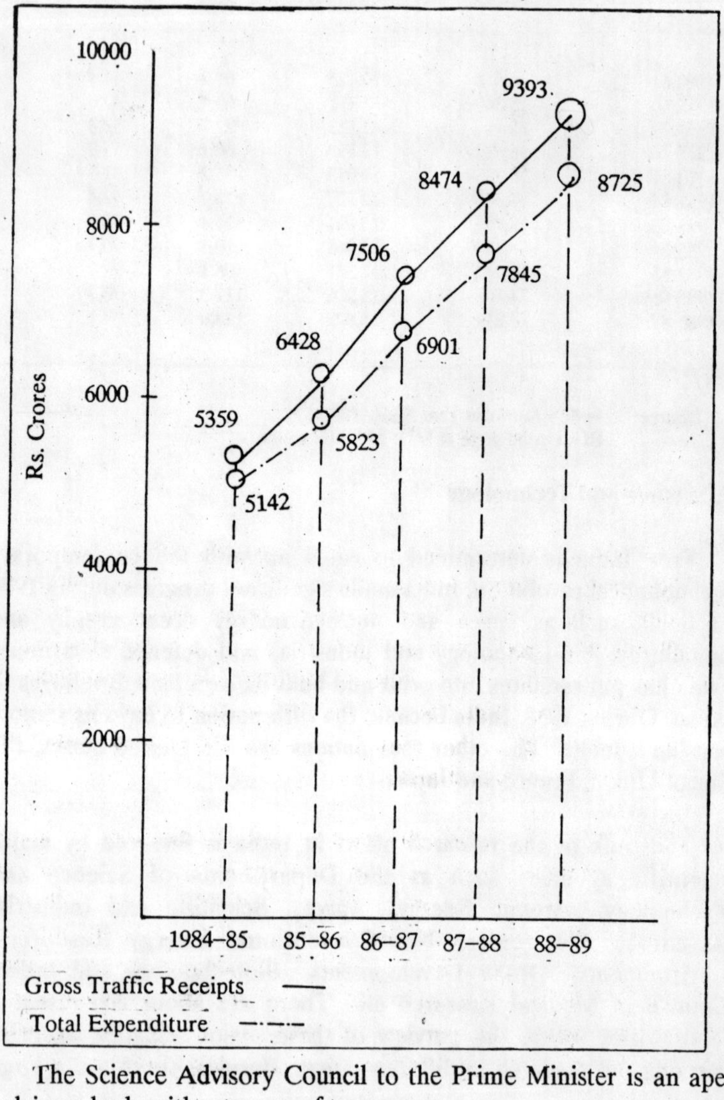

The Science Advisory Council to the Prime Minister is an apex advisory body with a tenure of two years.

The Government of India's Science Policy is based on the Scientific Policy Resolution adopted by the Parliament in March 1958. The Department of Science and Technology (DST) was set up in 1971. The Technology Police Statement was announced in January 1983.

Antarctia Expedition

Antarctia, the frozen continent, is considered as common heritage of mankind and an ideal global laboratory. Since 1981, the Government of India has successfully launched seven scientific research expeditions with 141 scientists and 342 logistic personnel participating in the expedition. The seventh expedition returned to Goa in March 1988 after staying for seventy days in Antarctia.

Launching of Satellite

The Rs. 650 million, 975 kg. snow covered satellite was shot into space after a launch by the Soviet Vostok rocket from the Soviet cosmodrome at Baikonour at 12 hours and 13 minutes and 30 seconds (I.S.T.) on March 17. The satellite which went into a polar sum-synchronous orbit, was the heaviest of the seven indigenous satellites launched so far.

India's Multipurpose INSAT-C

After the failure of two successive ASLV rocket launches on March 24, 1987 and July 13, 1988, our scientists were successful in the launching of India's multipurpose INSAT-C, on July 22. It was put in orbit by an Ariane-3 rocket of European Space Agency (ESA) from Kourou in French Guyana.

CHAPTER 12

MAIN EVENTS OF THE YEAR

1. Cultural Exchange

The year long festival of the Soviet Union in India November 21, 1987 to November 1988, formed the largest – ever cultural exchange between two countries. Over 3,000 Soviet performers covered 150 cities and performed 1,019 shows. It was held to reciprocate the year long festival of India in the U.S.S.R.

2. Defence

India became the fourth country in the Third World, next to China, Brazil and Argentina to indigenously produce armed vehicles, missiles, ships and war planes - the four major categories of weapons.

The first indigenously assembled new battle tank T-72M rolled out of the project complex of the Heavy Vehicles Factory (HVF) in Avadi (Madras) in January. The battle tank was named as 'Ajay' (Invincible)

INS Chakra our first nuclear propelled submarine leased from the Soviet Union was inducted into our fleet on February 3. There is no simulation of nuclear weapons on board the submarine. It is equipped for training and self-defence.

With the Commissioning of India's first nuclear powered submarines at the Eastern Noval Command in Visakhapatnam on February 3, 1988, India joined the maritime nuclear powers. With the leasing of this submarine by the Soviet Union, the Indian Navy became the sixth maritime force in the world and the first in Asia to possess such a nuclear – propelled boat.

India successfully test fired a new generation 250 km range *Prithvi* surface to surface missile from the Sriharikota space station in Andhra Pradesh on Feburary 25.

Fig. XII.1

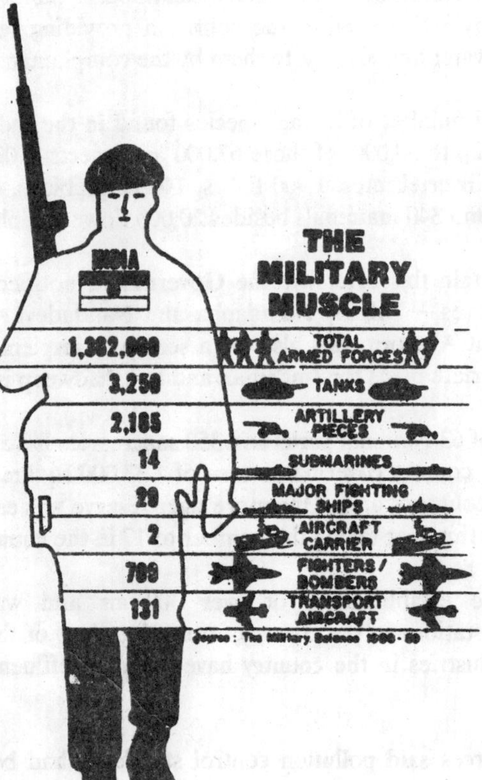

3. Earthquake

The one minute massive earthquake with its epicentre about 70 to 80 km. North-East of Darhbanga in Bihar that rocked the region in the early hours of August 21 was the strongest recorded in the sub-Himalayan terrain since the quake on January 15, 1934.

4. Environmental Conservation

Among the legislations of the year, the amendment to 1974 Water and Air Pollution Control Act gives more powers to the State Pollution Control boards including ordering of closure of erring industries, besides making punishment tougher.

About 67 laboratories have been identified in the country which are bound by laws to oblige the courts in providing results of the samples of water and air sent to them by the complainants.

The total number of animal species found in the Indian subcontinent adds up to 80,000; of these 67,000 are insects, 1,000 molluscs, 6,500 other invertebrates, 1,400 fishes, 140 amphibians, 420 reptiles, 1,200 birds and 340 mammals besides 20,000 flowering plants.

To maintain this diversity, the Government notified three biosphere reserves – Nilgiri, Namdapha and Nandadevi – An Island Development Authority has also been set up to implement ecologically appropriate plans for Andaman and Lakshadweep islands.

A total of 63 National parks and 358 sanctuaries have been established in the country covering an area of 1,33,000 sq. km, about four per cent of country's area. One more tiger reserve was established in Tamil Nadu this year taking the number to 17 in the country.

With the establishment of over 300 air and water quality monitoring stations in the country, more than half of the large and medium industries in the country have installed effluent treatment plants.

The sources said pollution control standards had been notified for 24 categories of industries and recently draft rules have been framed for controlling hazardous chemicals.

Five regional institutes have been set up in the country through the Indian Council for Forestry Research and Education.

To develop integrated subtainable development strategies for the Himalayas, "Gobind Ballabh Pant Himalalya Paryavaran Vikas

Sansthan" was established recently at Almora in Uttar Pradesh.

5. Exports of Gems and Jewels

(Rs. in crores)

Year	Exports
1985-86	1,502.65
1986-87 (p)	2,059.28
1987-88 (p)	2,613.50
1988-89 (p) (April-October)	2,449.00

(Source: Minister of Commerce, L.S., Uns. Q.1326, dated 18.11.88)

Export of Pepper from India from 1.4.88. to 31.10.88

Country	Qty. M. Tons.
USSR	5163
USA	3865
GDR (West)	1296
Italy	1254
France	1217
Yugoslavia	1101
Saudi Arabia	1078
Libya	1023
Netherlands	909
Egypt	856
GDR (East)	719
Canada	704
Tunisia	605
UAE	644
UK	473
Bulgaria	465
Others	4123
Total	25495

Source: Figures are provisional.
(*Minister of Commerce, L.S., Uns. Q. 3089, dated 2-12-88*)

6. Finance Commission (Ninth)

The setting up of a Finance Commission once every five years for the devolution of Central tax proceeds to the States is a constitutional requirement. In fulfilling this constitutional obligation, the Ninth Finance Commission, constituted by the President on June 17, 1987, was entrusted with the onerous task of adopting a normative approach in assessing the receipts and expenditure on revenue account of the States and the Centre.

In its first report, covering the period 1989-90, the Commission adopted the normative approach selectively. The commission estimated the resource transfers to the States for 1989-90, the terminal year of the Seventh Plan, to be of the order of Rs. 13,662 crore. The total volume of transfer, according to the report, is higher than what the States were receiving in 1988-89. The Commissison has stressed the need for fiscal discipline at the two levels of the Government and said that in allowing for increased transfer of resources to the states, it had kept in mind the financial needs and resources of the Centre.

It suggested that during 1989-90 the States should continue to receive 85 per cent of the proceeds from Income tax. As for the excise duties, the existing arrangement under which 45 per cent of the net proceeds of shareable excise duties is distributed among the states, would continue in 1989-90. No departure has been contemplated in the existing practice in regard to the devolution of other taxes and grants.

7. Housing

A National Housing Policy was presented in Parliament on November 22, 1988. There was an estimated all India Housing shortage of 28.5 million according to the National Building Organisation Projection based on the 1981 census. Among other things, the policy intends to upgrade all Kutcha houses in urban areas along with improving the housing conditions of slum dwellers, squatters, and other economically weaker sections.

8. Judiciary

Court cases

A total of 82,712 cases were pending in Delhi High Court as on June 30, 1988.

Supreme Court

There were 26 posts of Judges in the Supreme Court in the year 1988

9. Members of Parliament–Salaries

The salary of a Member of Parliament was raised from Rs.1000 to Rs.1500 a month and daily allowance was doubled from Rs.150 in 1988.

10. Polity

Tamil Nadu

Mrs. Janaki Ramchandran became the Chief Minister of Tamil Nadu on January 7, after the demise of her husband M.G. Ramchandra who was the Chief Minister. However, the Ministry was very shortlived and President's rule was promulgated in the State on January 22, 1988. In the State Assembly Elections held on January 21, 1989, the D.M.K. under the leadership of Karunanidhi, won an absolute majority.

Nagaland

Nagaland was put under President's rule on August 7 and Ministry was dissolved. The Congress (I) under the leadership of S.C. Jamer formed the Ministry on January 24, 1989 after its victory in the elections held on January 21, 1989.

Meghalaya

Congress I, Ministry was formed in Meghalaya on February 8.

Madhya Pradesh

Motilal Vohra resigned as Chief Minister of Madhya Pradesh and Arjun Singh became the CM on February 13. Almost after a year Arjun Singh had to resign because of a High Court Judgement and Moti Lal Vohra, Union Health Minister took the oath of office as Chief Minister on January 25, 1989.

Mizoram

Mizoram came under the President's rule on September 7, and Laldenga Ministry came to an end. Lalthanhawala of the Congress I, formed the Ministry on January 23, 1989 after its victory in the Assembly Elections; the Mizo National Front (MNF) headed by former Chief Ministry Laldenga was defeated. Laldenga had come to power in 1986 after the Mizo peace accord.

Punjab

The Operation Black Thunder which began in Amritsar on May 9, to clear the Golden Temple of with the terrorist ended on May 18, with the surrender of all terrorists inside the Golden Tample.

Election

The Congress I, suffered a set back in the by-election of 11 Assembly and 7 Lok Sabha Constituencies, which were held on June 16, 1988. It suffered a major defeat in the prestigious Allahabad Constituency which was won by Vishwanath Pratap Singh, the Jan Morcha leader who had resigned from the Lok Sabha and the Congress I.

U.P. and Maharashtra

On June 24, N.D. Tiwari became the new Chief Minister of U.P. in place of B.B. Singh and Sharad Powar was elected the new Chief Minister of Maharashtra in place of S.B. Chawan who resigned.

Bofors Probe

On July 5, twenty-four opposition leaders representing almost all parties in Parliament called on the President and submitted a memorandum to advise the Government to institute a thorough and impartial inquiry into Bofors in view of the additional disclosers made by *The Hindu* in a series of documents published in June.

Karnataka

Ramakrishna Hedge, the Chief Minister of Karnataka, resigned from office on August 11, owing moral responsibility for alleged tapping of telephones in the State. S.R. Bommai of the outgoing Hedge Cobinet became the Chief Minister of the State on August 13.

Tripura

The memorandam of settlement signed on August 12, at New Delhi by the Union and the Tripura Government with the Tripura National Volunteers (TNV) marked the end of violence in State's political history. The TNV which was formed on December 21, 1978 by Hrang Khawl agreed not to resort to violence. The Government agreed to make suitable consitutional amendments to raise the member of seats reserved for the Scheduled Tribes in the Tripura Assembly from 17 to 20.

Gorkha Agreement

Twenty eight months of agitation, tension and violence which accounted for the loss of hundreds of innocent lives come to a happy end on August 22, with the signing of an agreement signed at Darjeeling with the West Bengal Government and the Gorkha National Liberation Front (GNLF). The Darjeeling Accord provided for the setting up of the Gorkha Hill Council. An other agreement was signed in New Delhi on August 23 between GNLF and the Centre which dealt with issues like the citizenship. The Darjeeling Gorkha Hill Council was formed on December 26 under Subash Ghising

Defamation Bill

The Defamation Bill which provided that henceforth any false imputation against an individual, a company or an association or a collection of persons will be treated as an offence and those making the imputation will be liable for punishment was passed by the Lok Sabha on August 30.

The Defamation Bill was adopted by the Lok Sabha on August 29 despite a strong resistance by the opposition parties. All over the country the Press started a movement against the Bill and boycotted even the Press Conference of the Minister. The Bill was withdrawn on September 22.

National Front

The National Front, a combination of seven opposition parties was formed on September 17, with N.T. Rama Rao as the Chairman and V.P. Singh as the convenor. Thereafter a new party called Janta Dal came into being.

Prime Minister's Foreign Visits

Prime Minister Rajiv Gandhi vistied Syria, West Germany, New York and Hungary in June, Jordan, Yugoslavia, Spain and Turkey in July and China and Pakistan in December.

11. Postal and Railway Rates

With the commencement of the 1988-89 financial year on April 1, the increased postal and telecommunications, tariffs and increased railway fares came into force.

12. Rupee Value

(As on 31.12.88)

County	Currency	Unit	TT Selling Rates Rs.	TT Buying Rates Rs
Australia	Dollar	1	13.2159	13.0788
Austria	Schilling	100	1.2091	1.1925
Bahrain	Dinar	1	39.0026	38.9820
Bangladesh	Taka	100	47.4330	47.3826
Canada	Dollar	1	12.7281	12.5985
Denmark	Kroner	1	2.2011	2.1773
Egypt	Pound	1	6.9026	6.8528
France	Franc	1	2.5221	2.4600
Hong Kong	Dollar	1	1.9432	1.9239
Indonesia	Rupiah	100	0.0800	0.0700
Iran	Rial	100	21.5222	21.4526
Italy	Lira	100	1.0500	1.0300
Japan	Yen	100	12.2850	11.9760
Kenya	Shilling	1	0.7126	0.6928

Kuwait	Dinar	1	51.2328	51.1120
Malaysia	Dollar	1	5.6035	5.5468
Mauritius	Rupee	1	1.0300	1.0000
Nepal	Rupee	1	0.6720	0.6328
Netherlands	Guilder	1	7.5251	7.4442
Pakistan	Rupee	1	0.7928	0.7436
Singapore	Dollar	1	7.8158	7.7355
Spain	Peseta	1	0.1128	0.1009
Sri Lanka	Rupee	1	0.4300	0.4100
Sweden	Kroner	1	2.4705	2.4425
Switzerland	Franc	1	9.9996	9.8954
Tanzania	Shilling	1	0.1300	0.1000
Thailand	Baht	100	57.8128	57.6626
UK	Pound	1	27.2294	27.0893
USA	Dollar	1	15.1745	15.0263
UAE	Dirham	1	4.0000	3.9000
USSR	Rouble	1	18.2660	18.2000
W. Germany	Deutschmark	1	8.6133	8.3963

13. Security

The Government incurred more than Rs.8.39 crore during the last two years on the special protection group, which is concerned with the proximate security of the Prime Minister.

14. Strikes

The number of mandays lost due to strikes and lockouts increased from 32.74 million in 1986 to 35.36 million in 1987.

15. Woman

The National Perspective Plan for Woman (NPPW) 1988, for the first time since the 1976 National Plan of Action, presented a holistic approach to the development of women. It suggested a 30 per cent reservation for women. It provided for a Commission for Women's Rights to monitor the violation of laws.

Dowry Deaths

With 584 cases, Uttar Pradesh topped the list with a total of 1390 cases registered as dowry deaths in the country from January 1 to October 31, 1988. 229 cases were registered as dowry deaths in

Maharashtra, follwed by Karnataka 145, West Bengal (excluding Calcutta city) 83, Andhra Pradesh 72, Tamil Nadu 59, Punjab 30, Union Territory of Delhi 39. Dowry deaths registered during 1986 and 1987 were 1,319 and 1,418 respectively. These deaths took place despite the Dowry Prohibition (Amendment) Act, 1984 which came into force on October 2, 1985 covering all Indian nationals irrespective of their relgion.

In a landmark judgement the Supreme Court held in November, 1987 that the demand for dowry amounted to cruelty entitling a wife to get a decree for dissolution of marriage and that intention is not a necessary element to constitute cruelty in law

On June 24, 1987 the Union Government announced that if a case has been registered by the police against a Government servant in a dowry death case, he would be placed under suspension. If the Government servant is arrested in connection with the registration of the police case, he shall be placed under suspension irrespective of the period of his detention. If he is not arrested, he shall be placed under suspension immediately on submission of a police report to the magistrate if the prima-facie indicates that the offence has been committed by the Government servant. The gruesome suicide by three grown-up daughters named Poonam, Kamini and Alka of Gaya Prasad Sahu in Kanpur on February 3, 1988 shocked the entire nation.

16. Youth

The National Youth Week commenced on the 12th of January with the celebration of Swami Vivekananda's birthday. Prime Minister Rajiv Gandhi, on this occasion, exhorted the youth with a message from Swami Vivekananda, "Devote yourselves heart and soul to one principal duty, the duty of raising the masses of India, awakening them and uniting them".

APPENDICES

APPENDIX-I

CONCEPTS AND TECHNICAL TERMS

Absolute Poverty Level

That income level below which a minimum nutritionally adequate diet plus essential non-food requirements is not affordable.

Adult Literacy Rate (ALR)

Percentage of persons aged 15 and over who can read and write.

Child Malnutrition

Mild or moderate: between 60% and 80% of the desirable weight-for-age, severe less than 60% of the desirable weight-for-age.

Crude Birth Rate

Annual number of births per 1,000 population.

Crude Death Rate

Annual number of deaths per 1,000 population.

DPT

Diphtheria, pertussis (whooping cough) and tetanus.

GNP

Gross national product. Annual GNPs per capita are expressed in current United States dollars. GNP per capita growth rates are annual average growth rates that have been computed by fitting trend lines to the logarithmic values of GNP per capita at constant market prices for each year of the time period.

Infant Mortality Rate (IMR)

Annual number of deaths of infants under one year of age per 1,000 live births.

Life Expectancy at Birth

The number of years new-born children would live if subject to the mortality risks prevailing for the cross-section of population at the time of their birth.

ORS

Oral rehydration salts.

Primary and Secondary Enrolment Ratios

The gross enrolment ratio is the total number of children enrolled in a schooling level - whether or not they belong in the relevant age group for that level - expressed as a percentage of the total number of children in the relevant age group for that level. The net enrolment ratio is the total number of children enrolled in a schooling level who belong in the relevant age group, expressed as a percentage of the total number of children in that age group.

Under Five Mortality Rate (UFMR)

Annual number of deaths of children under 5 years of age per 1,000 live births.

APPENDIX-II

ECONOMIC SURVEY 1988-89

The pre-Budget Economic Survey for 1988-89 presented to Parliament on February 24, 1989 called for adoption by the Government of a composite package of measures for reducing the Centre's budgetary deficit which was posing a threat to the long-term stability of the economy.

This package, as reported, included strong curbs on the growth of current expenditure, steps to enhance buoyancy of tax revenues and measures aimed at broadening the effective base for direct taxation. The Survey pointed out that the programme for reducing the growth of Government expenditure must embrace several features, including elimination of all wasteful and low priority expenditures, moderation in salary and wage growth and limits on the growing bill of subsidies through better targetting of beneficiaries. Further, to moderate the growth in interest obligations of the Centre the scale of overall borrowing requirements will have to be contained.

The Survey also pointed out that though the economy recorded a high-growth rate of 9 per cent as againstt 3.6 per cent in 1987-88 and the rate of inflation had been pegged at 5 per cent as against the previous year's 10.6 per cent, the dificult balance of payments situation and continuing strain on public finance were plaguing the economy, adversely affecting both the short-term and the long-term stability of the economy.

The seriousness of the fiscal imbalance was apparent from the fact that by 1987-88, the gap between the gross capital formation out of the budgetary resources of the Central Government and the gross saving of the Centre had risen to over 9 per cent of GDP and public savings as a whole had fallen to 1.9 per cent of the GDP from a peak of 5.2 per cent in 1976-77. So, the Survey observed that a turn-around in public savings performance was crucial for financing the levels of public investment necessary for continued strong economic growth in medium term.

The Survey revealed that this turn-around must come from both an improvement in the budgetary balances of the Central and the State Governments as well as increased surplus generation by the public sector enterprises. It pointed out that the restoration of a better balance between the Government's revenue and expenditure was not only essential for bringing about the desired improvement in the public sector savings performance but also for enhancing future prospects of price stability. It pointed out that a reduction in the underlying average rate of inflation in the medium term was likely to require a reduction in the average rate of growth of money supply which in turn would entail moderation in the budget deficit.

Despite 24 per cent rise in exports during April-December 1988, the trade deficit went up during the period by Rs. 1,688 crore as the imports went up by 27.4 per cent and this had a definite impact on the foreign exchange reserves which recorded a fall by Rs. 1,483 crore in January 1989 as against the corresponding month of 1988. The adverse factors contributing to the difficult balance of payments position included the deceleration in indigenous oil production, protectionist trends in international trade, uncertainties with respect to flow of remittances from Indians working abroad and bunching of repayment obligations of past loans from the International Monetary Fund.

A further disquieting feature of the economy was the decline in the rate of domestic savings, which as a proportion of gross domestic product (GDP) new series declined from 21.6 per cent in 1986-87 to 20.2 per cent in 1987-88. The rate of gross capital formation also fell from 23.4 per cent in 1986-87 to 22.1 per cent in 1987-88. Capital inflow from abroad as a proportion of GDP increased from 1.7 per cent in 1986-87 to 1.9 per cent in 1987-88, indicating a positive development.

The high GDP growth rate in 1988-89 was possible owing to the 17 per cent increase in the agricultural production following good monsoons during the year and the rise in industrial production by about 8 per cent. In 1987-88, which was the year of drought, agricultural production fell by 2 per cent while industrial production rose by 7.5 per cent. According to the Survey, such good performance was attributable to basic policy reforms which promoted efficient competition and to long-term changes in the industrial structure which made the industrial sector less sensitive to fluctuations in agricultural production.

The Survey brought to light that the major challenges of economic management in 1988 come from a difficult balance of payments situation and the continuing strain on public finance. On the external payments front, the effect of several adverse medium-term factors aggravated during the year 1988 by the surge in imports. On the resources front, the challenge had been one of adequately financing plan expenditure in a non-inflationary manner in order to maintain the momentum of economic recovery while at the same time accommodating the increase in major items in expenditure, such as interest payments, subsidies and defence expenditure.

The Survey expected that as regards agriculture, the production in foodgrains might exceed the target of 166 million tonnes and the Survey claimed that the comprehensive measures introduced in 1987 in order to contain the impact of the drought hastened the process of quick recovery and it was possible to take full advantage of the good monsoon in 1988 for optimising production under the special production programme for foodgrains. High levels of production had also been recorded in cotton, surgarcane and especially oilseeds.

The Survey observed that, recent policy initiatives in oilseeds and edible oils succeeded in more than halving the level of edible oils imports within a year. However it pointed out that the stagnation in the production of most pulses was a cause for serious concern since pulses form a major source of protein for Indian consumers.

Regarding industry and infrastructure, the Survey revealed that in earlier post-drought years, industrial growth suffered from the adverse spillover effects of drought. During 1988-89, however, industrial production recorded strong growth from the beginning of the year and the growth rate was over 9 per cent up to November

1988. High industrial growth for the fifth year in succession reflected the positive effects of an on going process of industrial policy reforms aimed at promoting competitivenes, better capacity utilisation and cost efficiency in the industrial sector.

The Survey pointed out that a number of such policy initiatives undertaken during the past year and some of these new measures would facilitate expansion of production within existing capacities while others were directed at encouraging the creation of new capacities. Important steps were taken to simplify the administration of industrial policy and eliminate procedural impediments. The good performance of industry and advances in policy reforms and fresh fiscal concessions extended during 1988 had been reflected in the buoyant stock market.

Regarding inflation and price management, Survey claimed that the containment of inflation during the last two years had been possible mainly on account of timely introduction of a range of anti-inflationary measures during the previous year. On the demand side, these included a whole range of steps aimed at financing relief measures without allowing any undue increase in the budget defict and this facilitated the implementation of the policy of restrained money supply growth. Similarly, on the supply side, the Government ensured adequate availability of foodgrains and other essential commodities through a vastly expanded public distribution system, the various employment programmes and relief operations. Aslo, wherever necessary, additional imports were undertaken to maintain adequate supplies as in the case of edible oils and pulses. A little over two million tonnes of foodgrains were imported in order to maintain adequate food security.

As regards the fiscal and monetary policies of the Government, the Survey stated that the overall fiscal policy stance during the year had been supported by a monetary policy which sought to provide adequate credit for accommodating the strong resurgence of growth while at the same time maintaining restraint in the growth of liquiditty in the system. Thus M3 growth had been contained at around 15 per cent up to the middle of January and the banks were able to accommodate a larger flow of non-food credit in 1988-89 compared with 1987-88 because of a substantial decline in food credit.

The Survey reported a number of important developments relating to the interest rate structure and related institutional arrangements. The most important among these were the replacement of a ceiling interest rate for trade and industry by a floor rate and the termination of the credit authorisation scheme, which required prior sanction of credit limits for bulk advances to the non-food commercial sector. Many institutional developments in the financial sector included the establishment of the National Housing Bank, the Discount and Finance House of India, the Security Exchange Board of India and the launching of the Credit Rating and Investment Services of India Ltd.

According to the Survey, the relatively comfortable situation in foodgrains and edible oils in 1988 could provide an appropriate background for framing a policy of food management for the Eighth Plan period and beyond. It pointed out that the food policy perspectives for the future would have to take into account the situation under which, a substantial proportion of the population, remains undernourished and below the poverty line.

The Survey, therefore, urged that adequate coverage of the genuinely vulnerable population under existing constraints of foodgrains availability and financial resources would require subsidised food supplies to be more carefully targeted. At the same time, the food management policy, according to the Survey, should aim at containing the open market prices of foodgrains and edible oils within a reasonable limit through market intervention operations by appropriate agencies for the protection of the consumers in general.

The Survey reported that according to the quick estimates the National Income at 1980-81 prices was Rs. 150,573 crore in 1987-88 and Rs. 257,813 crore at the currentt prices. Likewise per capita income was Rs. 1918.1 and 3284.2 respectively.

APPENDIX-III

BUDGET 1989-1990

Main Objectives of the Budget

The budget is oriented to the following ends:
- promoting productive employment,
- protecting the consumption standards of the poor,
- providing some relief to middle income taxpayers,
- maintaining the tempo of industrial modernisation and growth,
- containing the budget deficit for 1989-90.

Budget at a glance

(In crores of Rupees)

	1987-88 Actuals	1988-89 Budget estimates	1988-89 Revised estimates	1989-90 Budget estimates
Revenue	37226	42798	43135	52630
Capital Receipts	22026	23278	24708	22194
TOTAL RECEPTS	59252	66076	67843	74824
Non-Plan Expenditure	40869	47846	48877	54347
Plan Expenditure	24199	25714	26906	27814
TOTAL EXPENDITURE	65068	73560	75783	82161
Revenue Expenditure	46363	52640	54165	59642
Capital Expenditure	18705	20920	21618	22519
Revenue Deficit	9137	9842	11030	7012
OVERALL DEFICIT	5816	7484	7940	7337
Increase in net RBI Credit to Central Government*	6559	7484	8200	7337**

* Including other variations in Reserve Bank of India's credit to Central Government.

** Not independently estimated.

Rupee : Revenue – Expenditure

Revenue	Paise	Expenditure	Paise
Excise	24	Central Plan	18
Customs	19	Interest	18
Internal borrowings	16	Defence	14
Non-tax revenue	14	Share of taxes	13
Deficit	8	Other non-Plan expenditure	14
Other capital receipts	4	State & UT Plan assistance	11
Corporation tax	5	Subsidies	9
Income tax	5	Non-Plan assistance	3
External assistance	4		
Other taxes	1		

Additional Taxation

Year	Rs. in crores
1980-81	282
1981-82	271
1982-83	533
1983-84	716
1984-85	273
1985-86	431
1986-87	488
1987-88	514
1988-89	615
1989-90	1287

Year	Overall Deficit (Rs. in crores)
1980-81	2477
1981-82	1400
1982-83	1655 *
1983-84	1416 *
1984-85	3745
1985-86	5315 *
1986-87	8261
1987-88	5816
1988-89 (Revised)	7940
1989-90 (Budget)	7337

(* Excludes loans of Rs. 1743 crore in 1982-83, Rs. 400 crores in 1983-84 and Rs. 1628 crores in 1985-86 granted to States to clear their Overdrafts with the Reserve Bank of India).

Levies

* Eight per cent income-tax surcharge on incomes above Rs. 50,000 from assessment year 1990-91.
* Expenditure tax, applicable to certain hotels, up from 10 per cent to 20 per cent.
* Five per cent hike in the specific duty rates of a large number of commodities barring articles of mass consumption.
* Cigarettes: Non-filter cigarettes of length up to 60mm to carry excise duty of Rs. 1 per packet of 10. Filter cigarettes of length above 70mm will carry higher duty.
* Pan masala: Duty on non-tobacco pan masala in the two existing slabs of Rs. 10 and Rs. 20 a kg doubled. Excise on pan masala containing tobacco up from 25 per cent to 30 per cent.
* Inland Air Travel Tax to be levied at the rate of 10 per cent of basic fare.
* Foreign Travel Tax to be raised from Rs. 50 to Rs. 150 for neighbouring countries and from Rs. 100 to Rs. 300 for travel to the other countries.

* Automobiles: Concessional duty on fuel-efficient cars discontinued. Uniform levy of 35 per cent to be imposed on all cars, vans and jeeps.
* Two-wheelers: Excise duty on two-wheelers between 50cc and 100cc up by 5 per cent. Duty on two-wheelers above 150cc raised to 30 per cent
* Electronics: Duty on colour TV sets raised from Rs. 1,500 to Rs. 2,250 for sets without remote control, to Rs. 2,500 for sets with remote control, and to Rs, 4,000 for sets with "picture in picture" facility. Duty on black and white sets of screen size exceeding 36 cm up from Rs. 300 to Rs. 500 per set; picture tube of sets with screen size between 15 cm and 36 cm raised by Rs. 200 per tube, but the sets themselves will continue to be exempted from excise duty.
* Duty on computers up from 10 per cent to 15 per cent. Benefits of general scheme of exemption for small-scale sector withdrawn.
* Radios, two-in-ones, cassette recorders and musical systems to have uniform rate of 20 per cent as against the present 15 per cent or 20 per cent.
* Iron and steel items: Duty on pig iron up from Rs. 80 to Rs. 200 per tonne. Duty on steel ingots, billets, bars and rods up from Rs. 365 to Rs. 500 a tonne. Duty on hot rolled sheets and strips up from Rs. 500 to Rs. 700 a tonne, and on cold rolled flat products up from Rs. 715 to Rs. 900 per tonne. Duty on stainless steel ingots and semi-finished products raised to Rs. 1,000 per tonne, and on certain cold-rolled products, castings and forgings to Rs. 1,500 per tonne.
* Duty on aluminium ingots and wire-rods up by 2 per cent plus Rs. 2,500 per tonne. Duty on most of the dutiabe downstream products raised by 10 per cent.
* Basic customs duty on glazed news-print raised from Rs. 550 per tonne to 30 per cent ad valorem.
* Watches and watch components will attract 5 per cent excise duty as against 2 per cent so far.

Reliefs

* Rate of income-tax in the entry slab of Rs. 18,000-25,000 reduced from 25 per cent to 20 per cent for individuals, unregistered firms and non-specified HUFs.

* Drought surcharge of five per cent on income-tax and 10 per cent on wealth tax withdrawn.
* Standard deduction of Rs. 12,000 or 33.33 per cent, whichever is less, on family pensions received by widows/heirs.
* Deduction of Rs. 15,000, available to permanently physically handicapped persons to be extended to the mentally retarded persons.
* Profession Tax, imposed by State Government on salaries, to be allowed as deduction in computing total income for tax purposes.
* Investments in units of any scheme of the Unit Trust of India eligible for deduction under Section 80CC, if the funds of such scheme are invested in the eligible issue of capital.
* Annuity plans of LIC exempted from wealth tax.
* Agro-based products: Excise duty on skimmed milk powder and condensed milk reduced from 15 per cent to 10 per cent, but duty exemption of skimmed milk powder in one kg pack withdrawn.
* "Namkeens" such as bhujiyas and chabna and specified ready-to-cook mixes such as idli-mix and vada-mix fully exempted from excise duty.
* Excise duty on preparations of fish, meat, tapioca and sago in units containers down from 15 to 10 per cent.
* Full excise duty concession on varieties of paper and paper board containing not less than 75 per cent of pulp made from raw jute or mesta.
* Duty on synthetic organic dyestuffs reduced from 35 per cent to 30 per cent.
* Duty on cement manufactured by units using vertical shaft kiln reduced by Rs. 100 per tonne.
* Duty concession for the capital goods industry for import of machinery to upgrade technology extended to four more sectors: cutting tools, commercial tool rooms, textile machinery and paper machinery. Rate of import duty on general projects and machinery down from 90 to 80 per cent. Corresponding reduction in duty on components.
* Interest on investments in a new deposit scheme for retiring employees, being introduced, will be exempt from income-tax provided the retirement benefit is invested in full or in part for a block period of three years. Present ceiling of exemption of

wealth up to Rs. 5 lakh in specified forms will not apply to such deposits.

* Jute yarn supplied to a registered handloom co-operative society or an organisation set up or approved by the Government will be exempt from excise duty.
* Synthetic shoddy blankets of value up to Rs. 60 per sq metre exempt from excise duty.
* Concessional rate of duty to be extended to some more items of machinery used in the food processing and packaging industry: 15 per cent concessional duty on refrigerating appliances and machinery used in refrigerated vans transporting food and diary products.

Sector - Wise Plan Outlay

(Rupees in Crores)

Sector	1988-89 Budget Estimates	1988-89 Revised Estimates	1989-90 Budget Estimates
Agriculture	1078	1290	1203
Rural Development	1762	1759	1762
Irrigation and Flood control	217	217	205
Energy	9128	9100	1227
Industries and Minerals	4816	5585	5934
Transport	5575	5555	6296
Communications	1820	2311	2858
Science, Technology and Environment	751	749	752
Social Services*	3269	3299	3396
Others	299	301	813
Total	28715	30166	34446
	410	410	410

* Includes Accelerated Rural Water Supply Programme)

Expenditure on Defence

Year	Expenditure in Rs. Crores
1985-86	7,987
1986-87	10,477
1987-88	11,968
1988-89 (Revised Estimates)	13,200
1989-90 (Budget Estimates)	13,000

Excise Revenue

Year	Revenue in Rs. Crores
1985-1986	12956
1986-1987	14470
1987-1988	16426
1988-1989 (Revised estimates)	18547
1989-1989-90 (Budget estimates)	21910

Government Borrowings (Interest)

Year	Interest Rs. in Crores
1980-81	2604
1981-82	3195
1982-83	3938
1983-84	4796
1984-85	5974
1985-86	7503
1986-87	9236
1987-88	11236
1988-89 (Revised Estimates)	14150
1989-90 (Budget Estimates)	17000

APPENDIX-IV

INSTITUTIONS OF NATIONAL IMPORTANCE

Agriculture

Central Inland Fisheries Research Institute, Calcutta.
Nautical Engineering Training, Cochin.
Forest Research Institute and Colleges, Dehradun.
Indian Agricultural Research Institute, New Delhi.
Indian Agricultural Statistics Research Institute, New Delhi.
Indian Council of Agricultural Research, New Delhi.
Indian Society of Agricultural Economics, Bombay.
Indian Veterinary Research Institute, Izatnagar.
Indira Gandhi National Forest Academy, Dehradun.
National Dairy Research Institute, Karnal.
National Sugar Institute, Kanpur.
Rubber Board and Rubber Research Institute of India, Kottayam.

Art and Architecture

Allahabad Museum, Allahabad.
Archaeological Survey of India, New Delhi.
Centre for Cultural Resources and Training, New Delhi.
Indian Museum, Calcutta.
Indira Gandhi National Centre for Arts, New Delhi.
Indira Sangeet Vishwavidyalaya, Khairagarh.
Lalit Kala Academy (National Academy of Fine Arts), New Delhi.
National Gallary of Modern Art, New Delhi.
National Museum of India, New Delhi.
National Research Laboratory for Conservation of Cultural Property, Lucknow.
National School of Drama, New Delhi.
Nehru Memorial Museum and Library, New Delhi.

Rashtriya Manav Sangrahalaya (National Museum of Man), Bhopal.
Sahitya Akademi (National Academy of Cultures), New Delhi.
Salarjung Museum, Hyderabad.
Sangeet Natak Academy (National Academy of Music, Dance and Drama), New Delhi.
Sarnath Museum, Varanasi.
Victoria Memorial Hall, Calcutta.

Defence

Air Force Academy, Hyderabad.
Air Force Administrative College, Coimbatore.
Armed Forces Medical College, Pune.
College of Combat, Mhow.
Defence Institute of Physiology and Allied Sciences, New Delhi.
Defence Scientific Information and Documentation Centre, New Delhi.
Defence Services Officers Institute, New Delhi.
Indian Military Academy, Dehradun.
I.N.S. Chilka, near Bhubaneswar.
Institute of Defence Studies and Analysis, New Delhi.
National Defence Academy, Khadakvasala.
National Defence College, New Delhi.
Naval Academy, Co-Chin.
Officers Training School, Madras.
Rashtriya Indian Military College, Dehradun.

Employment and Training

Central Institute of Research and Training in Employment Services, New Delhi.
Institute of Secretariat Training and Management, New Delhi.
Public Enterprise Selection Board, New Delhi.
Staff Selection Commission, New Delhi.
Union Public Service Commission, New Delhi.

Health

All India Institute of Medical Sciences, New Delhi.
B.M. Institute of Mental Health, Ahmedabad.

Central Council of Indian Medicine, New Delhi.
Indian Council of Medical Research, New Delhi.
National Institute of Communicable Diseases, Delhi.
National Institute of Health and Communicable Diseases, New Delhi.
National Institute of Health and Family Welfare, New Delhi.
National Institute of Nutrition, Hyderabad.
Vallabhbhai Patel Chest Institute, Delhi.

Languages

Anjuman-i-Islam Urdu Research Institute, Bombay.
Bureau of Promotion of Urdu, New Delhi.
Central Hindi Directorate, New Delhi.
Central Institute of English and Foreign Languages, Hyderabad.
Central Institute of Higher Tibetan Studies, Varanasi.
Central Institute of Indian Languages, Mysore.
Kendriya Hindi Sansthan, Agra.
Rashtriya Sanskrit Sansthan, New Delhi.
School of Buddhist Philosophy, Leh.
Sikkim Research Institute of Tibetology, Gangtok.

Libraries

Adyar Library and Research Centre, Adyar, Madras.
Central Library, Bombay.
Central Reference Library, Calcutta.
Central Secretariat Library, New Delhi.
Connemara (State Central) Public Library, Madras.
Delhi Public Library, Delhi.
Government Oriental Manuscript Library, Madras.
Khuda Baksh Oriental Public Library, Patna.
Library of Tibetan Works and Archives, Dharamsala.
National Archives of India, New Delhi.
National Library, Calcutta.
Oriental Research Library, Pune.
Oriental Research Library, Vadodara.
Raja Ram Mohan Roy Library Foundation, Calcutta.
Rampur Raza Library, Rampur.
Tamil Nadu Government Oriental Manuscripts Library, Madras.

Thanjavur Maharaja Serfoji's Saraswati Mahal Library, Thanjavur.
Visheshwarananda Vedic Research Institute Library, Hoshiarpur.

Social Sciences

Administrative Staff College of India, Hyderabad.
Anthropological Survey of India, Calcutta.
Archaeological Survey of India, New Delhi.
Asiatic Society, Calcutta.
Association of Indian Universities, New Delhi.
Bhandarkar Oriental Research Institute, Pune.
Central Board of Secondary Education, New Delhi.
Directorate of Adult Education, New Delhi.
Gokhale Institute of Politics and Economics, Pune.
India International Centre, New Delhi.
Indian Council of Applied Economic Research, New Delhi.
Indian Council of Historical Research, New Delhi.
Indian Council of Philosophical Research, New Delhi.
Indian Council of World Affairs, New Delhi.
Indian Law Institute, New Delhi.
Indian Statistical Institute, Calcutta.
Indian Institute of Public Administration, New Delhi.
Indian Institute of Advanced Study, Shimla.
L.N. Mishra Institute of Economic Development and Social Change, Patna.
Indira Gandhi National Open University, New Delhi.
Indian National Commission for Cooperation with UNESCO, New Delhi.
Kendriya Vidyalaya Sangathan, New Delhi.
Madras Institute of Development Studies, Madras.
National Book Trust, New Delhi.
National Council of Applied Economic Research, New Delhi.
National Council of Educational Research and Training, New Delhi.
National Institute of Basic Education, New Delhi.
National Institute of Educational Planning and Administration, New Delhi.
National Institute of Public Cooperation and Child Development, New Delhi.
National Institute of Rural Development, Hyderabad.
National Productivity Council, New Delhi.

National Labour Institute, New Delhi.
Navodaya Vidalaya Samiti, New Delhi.
Oriental Institute, Baroda.
Oriental Research Institute, Mysore.
University Grants Commission, New Delhi.
Visheshwara Nand Vedic Research Institute, Hoshiarpur.

Science and Technology

Bhabha Atomic Research Centre, Bombay.
Birla Research Institute for Applied Sciences, Birlagram, Nagda.
Central Electronic Engineering Research Institute, New Delhi.
Central Electronic Limited, New Delhi.
Central Leather Research Institute, Madras.
Central Road Research Institute, New Delhi.
Central Mining Research Institute, Dhanbad.
Centre for Advanced Technology, Indore.
Council of Scientific and Industrial Research, New Delhi.
High Altitude Research Laboratory of BARC, Gulmarg.
Indian Academy of Sciences, Bangalore.
Indian Institute of Remote Sensing, Dehradun.
Indian National Science Academy, New Delhi.
Institute of Mathematical Sciences, Madras.
Institute of Physics, Bhubaneshwar.
ISRO Satellite Centre, Bangalore.
Metrological Data Utilisation Centre, New Delhi.
National Aeronautical Laboratory, Bangalore.
National Atlas and Thematic Mapping Organisation, New Delhi.
National Botanical Research Institute, Calcutta.
National Environmental Engineering Research Institute, Nagpur.
National Physical Laboratory, Delhi.
Nuclear Research Laboratory, Sri Nagar.
Nuclear Atomic Power Station, Tarapur.
Physical Research Laboratory, Ahmedabad.
Raman Research Institute, Bangalore.
Saha Institute of Nuclear Physics, Calcutta.
Solar Observatory, Udaipur.
Tata Institute of Fundamental Research, Bombay.
Variable Energy Cyclortorn Centre, Calcutta.
Vikram Sarabhai Space Centre, Trivandrum.
Zoological Survey of India, Calcutta.

APPENDIX-V

REFERENCE SOURCES

Adiseshiah, Malcolm, S., (1988), *Mid-year review of the Indian economy*, 1987-1988, New Delhi, Lancer International, 184p.

Aggarwal, J.C. and Agrawal, S.P., (1989), *National Policy on Education*, New Delhi, Concept Publishing Company, 153p.

Agrawal, S.P. ed., *India Since Independence*, New Delhi, Publication Division Ministry of Information and Broadcasting, 137p.

Bagchi, Amiya Kumar, ed. (1988), *Economy, society and polity : Essays in the political economy of Indian planning*, Calcutta, Oxford, 271p.

Bhadouria, B.P.H., ed. (1988), *Decentralised planning for development in India : Essays in honour of Prof. K.C.G. Seth*, Delhi, Commonwealth, xvi. 375p.

Chaturvedi, S.K., (1988), *Rural policing in India*, Delhi, B.R. Pub., xix, 176p.

Chaudhary, C.M., (1988), *Monetary policy in India*, Jaipur, National, viii, 196p.

Chopra, R.N., (1988), *Food policy in India : a survey*, New Delhi, Intellectual, xii, 414p.

Competition success review, India (1989), Annual review. ed by S.K. Sachdeva, New Delhi, Competition Review Pvt. Ltd., 446 p.

Creating a better climate for private enterprise : World Development Annual Report, 1987, N.Y., UNPD.

Das, Hari Hara and Das, Sasmita, (1988), *Indian government and politics*, Delhi, Discovery, vi, 359p.

Dobey, Kamala Kant and Singh, Alok Kumar, eds. (1988), *Urban environment in India : Problems and prospects*, New Delhi, Inter-India.

Etienne, Gilbert, (1988), *Food and poverty : India's half won battle*, New Delhi, Sage, 272p.

Gaur, Madan, (1988), *India : 40 years after independence*, Bombay, Press and Publicity Syndicate of India, 380p.

Goyal, R.P., (1988) *Marriage age in India*, Delhi, B.R. Pub., xii, 303p.

Grover, Verinder, ed. (1988), *Elections and politics in India*, New Delhi, Deep & Deep, 570p.

Haksar, Ajit N., (1988), *Political economic management of India, by India, for India : Creation of Wealth from Public Investment*, New Delhi, Vikas, xvi, 473p.

Hasnain, Nadeen, (1988), *Readings in Indian anthropology*, New Delhi, Harnam, viii, 152p.

Agrawal, A.N., Varma, H.O. and R.C. Gupta, (1988), *India : Economic information yearbook, 1988-89*, New Delhi, National, 293p.

India. National Sample Survey Organisation, (1987), Report on the third quinquennial survey on employment - Survey results, New Delhi, Dept. of Statistics, v.p. (Thirty eighth round, January-December 1983) Number 341.

Joshi, Kiran M., (1988), *Inflation, consumption and saving behaviour in India*, New Delhi, Anmol, 204p.

Kapila, Uma, ed., (1988), *Indian economy since independence*. Delhi, Synapse. 2 vols.

Kuppuram, G., (1988), *India through the ages : History, art, culture and religion*, Delhi, 2 vols.

Manorama year book, (1988), *Kottayam*, Manorama Publishing House, 733+p.

Misra, Bidyadhar, (1988), *Village life in India : Past and Present*, Delhi, Ajanta, vi, 168p.

Padhy, K.S. amd Satapathy, Purna Chandra, (1989), *Tribal India*, New Delhi, Ashish, xiii, 143p.

Saraswathi, S., (1988), *Youth in India*, New Delhi, ICSSR, ix, 507p.

Shah Giri Raj, (1989), *Indian police : A retrospect*, New Delhi, Cosmo, vii, 224p.

The State of the World's Children, (1989), New York, Oxford University Press for UNICEF.

Tata Economic Consultancy Service, Bombay, (1987), *Statistical outline of India, 1987*: Bombay, Popular Prakashan, 1987.

Thakur, D., (1989), *Politics of land reforms in India*. New Delhi, Commonwealth, 1989. 212p.

Times of India directory and year book including who's who, (1988), ed. by Sham Lal, Bombay, Times of India Press, 992p.

Unesco facts and figures, (1987), Unesco.

U.N. Economic Commission for Asia and the Pacific, (1987), Economic and social survey of the Asia and Pacific, Bangkok, The Commission, 1988. 176p.

U.N. Economic Commission for Asia and the Pacific, (1987), Population of India. N.Y., U.N., 414p.
(Country monograph series : No. 10).

The World Bank Annual Report, (1988), Washington D.C.

World Health Statistics, Annual, (1987), Geneva, W.H.O.

Index